D1389111

COASTAL SHIPS

D. Ridley Chesterton

LONDON

IAN ALLAN

Published by Ian Allan Ltd., Shepperton, Surrey and printed in the United Kingdom by The Press at
Coombelands Ltd., Addlestone, Weybridge, Surrey.

PREFACE

This combined volume brings together under a single cover the ships previously listed in the smaller ABC's of Coastal Passenger and Cargo Ships, Foreign Coastal Freighters and Tugs. Included are all British and Irish vessels of over 200 tons employed on coastal services and on short seas routes from the North Sea and Scandinavian ports to Brest, a large selection of the major European-owned vessels engaged in similar trades, all British tugs of over 100 gross tons and many similar tugs engaged in coastal towing from North European ports. Opportunity has also been taken to include details of many sand carriers and dredgers which, although not coastal traders in the strict sense of word, nevertheless number among their ranks many vessels which once engaged in coastal trading including some of the oldest one-time coasters still afloat.

In general, the lists are restricted to vessels of over 200 gross tons, but in the case of British companies the names of smaller units are included in abbreviated form. As in previous editions, company titles have been simplified and a list of the abbreviations used in the tables will be found below.

Grateful acknowledgement is again made to the many shipping companies which have helped with information, to Lloyd's Register, and to those who have supplied photographs.

Abbreviations

COMPANY TITLES, etc.

M.S. = Motorship
Nav. = Navigation
Shpg. = Shipping
S.N. = Steam Navigation
S.P. = Steam Packet
S.S. = Steamship
Stm Shpg. = Steam Shipping
Tdg. = Trading

A note on certain foreign abbreviations is included in the introduction to that section.

TYPES OF MACHINERY, etc.

M = Diesel or I.C. engines
ME = As above, but with electric drive
RT = Combined steam reciprocating and turbine machinery
SR = Steam reciprocating, compound or triple expansion
ST = Steam turbines
TE = Steam turbines with electric drive

(A) = Engines aft

(2) = Twin screw

(3) = Triple screw

(PW) = Paddle Wheel

B = Brake or Shaft Horse Power

I = Indicated Horse Power (Usually reckoned as 87% of Brake Horse Power)

D = Displacement Tonnage (Used only in connection with certain Admiralty tugs)

Other notes and abbreviations relating to isolated fleet lists are explained in the context.

Note On Description Of Houseflags

It is not easy to describe in words a houseflag in such a way as to avoid possible misinterpretation.

Certain complicated designs embodying the armorial bearings of cities or dock authorities can only be described in very general terms. Where the phrase "the letters 'A B C D' in each corner" is used, it is intended to indicate that ONE letter only appears in each quarter, reading from top of the hoist and from hoist to fly.

In the case of very many of the smaller operators it has not proved possible to obtain details of any houseflag, if, in fact, one exists.

Hulls are black unless otherwise indicated.

INDEX

BRITISH
COASTAL SHIPS

[*John G. Callis*]

M.V. B.P. Supervisor. Shell Mex & B.P. Ltd.

INTRODUCTION

The following pages deal with all Coastal Passenger and Cargo Ships of over 200 gross tons registered under the British or Irish flags, together with all coastal tankers of similar dimensions and a representative list of sand-carriers and suction dredgers. These last, which do not fall strictly within the general category of the ships listed in the volume, are nevertheless included in response to many requests and not least in view of the fact that so many one-time coasting vessels, some of considerable age, are numbered among them. In general, the sphere of operations of the vessels listed may be described as the Coastal, Cross-Channel, and Short Sea routes between British and Irish ports and the Continent of Europe from Norway to Brest. In certain cases, however, notably Ellerman's Wilson Line, the General Steam Navigation Co., and others, vessels trade further afield to the Mediterranean and North African ports.

In the dimensional tables, the gross tonnage, service speed, and overall length are given, except in a few cases where the registered length, generally some 5 to 15 ft less, is given. Regular routes, whether passenger or cargo, are indicated, and although in general the vessels listed fully are restricted to those of over 200 gross tons, additional units of each fleet which are of smaller dimensions are given in abbreviated form.

Grateful acknowledgment is made to the many firms and individuals who have helped in the production of this volume, notably the Shipping Companies, Lloyd's Register, and the many who have supplied new photographs.

M.V. Irish Coast. Coast Lines Ltd.

ABERDEEN COAL & SHIPPING CO. LTD.

ABERDEEN

FUNNEL: *Black with white band between two red bands.*
HOUSEFLAG:

Name				Date	Tons Gross	Length (feet)	Breadth (feet)	Speed (knots)	Engines
Ferryhill	...	...	...	1946	567	175	28	10	M(A)

ABERDEEN STEAM NAVIGATION CO. LTD.
(COAST LINES GROUP)

ABERDEEN

FUNNEL: *Yellow with green band.*
HOUSEFLAG: *Divided vertically into blue, white and blue.*

Hadrian Coast	...	...	...	1942	692	210	33	11½	M(A)

ASSOCIATED HUMBER LINES, LTD.

HULL

FUNNEL: *Yellow with black top and black "AHL" on broad red band.*
HOUSEFLAG: *Blue with red letters "$A^H L$" on white disc.*
SERVICES: *Hull–Rotterdam (Passenger and cargo). Hull to Rotterdam, Antwerp and Hamburg. Goole to the above ports and to Ghent, Amsterdam, Bremen and Hamburg (Cargo, some with limited passenger accommodation).*

Bolton Abbey	...	...	...	1957	2,706	302	45	15½	M(A)
Darlington	...	...	...	1958	963	232	39	12½	M(A)
Leeds ...	...	...	...	1959	1,114	244	39	12½	M(A)
Melrose Abbey	...	...	...	1959	2,500	302	45	15½	M(A)
Wakefield	...	...	...	1958	1,113	244	39	12½	M(A)
Whitby Abbey	...	...	...	1954	1,197	256	39	12½	M(A)
York ...	...	...	...	1960	1,110	244	39	12½	M(A)

ASTORIA SHIPPING & TRADING CO. LTD.

WHITEHAVEN

See James Fisher & Sons, Ltd.

ATLANTIC STEAM NAVIGATION CO. LTD.

LONDON

FUNNEL: *Blue with black top separated by broad white band.*

HOUSEFLAG: *White swallowtail pennant, edged with blue in the fly.*

SERVICES: *Passenger and Car Ferry: Tilbury–Antwerp, Tilbury–Rotterdam, Preston–Larne, Preston–Belfast. Container Traffic: Preston–Drogheda*

Bardic Ferry	...	...	...	1957	2,550	338	53	14	M(2)
Cerdic Ferry...	...	...	...	1961	2,563	361	55	14	M(2)
Doric Ferry ...	...	...	...	1961	2,563	361	55	14	M(2)
Gaelic Ferry	...	...	...	1964	2,760	347	56	14	M(2)
Ionic Ferry ...	...	...	...	1963	2,548	339	53	14	M(2)
Ministry of Transport vessel chartered to the company:									
Empire Nordic	...	...	...	1945	4,157	348	54	10	SR(2A)

BELFAST STEAMSHIP CO. LTD.

(COAST LINES GROUP)

BELFAST

FUNNEL: *Red with black top.*

HOUSEFLAG: *Red pennant bearing a white ball or disc.*

SERVICES: *Passenger: Belfast–Liverpool (Night service). Cargo: Belfast to Liverpool and/or Manchester (Integrated with the Belfast, Mersey & Manchester S.S.Co.).*

*Ulster Monarch	...	...	...	1929	3,802	359	46	17	M(2)
Ulster Prince	...	...	...	1937	4,303	367	50	17	M(2)
Ulster Spinner	...	...	...	1942	507	201	30	10½	M(A)
Ulster Sportsman ...	...	...	...	1936	789	237	37	13½	M(A)

*2 funnels

BELFAST, MERSEY & MANCHESTER STEAMSHIP CO LTD.

FUNNEL: *Yellow with black top.*

HOUSEFLAG:

SERVICES: *See above.*

Brookmount...	...	...	...	1949	995	265	39	12	M(A)
Colebrook ...	...	...	...	1948	1,075	286	39	11	M(A)
Mountstewart ...	...	...	...	1955	892	225	36	11	M(A)
Stormont ...	...	...	...	1954	906	225	36	11	M(A)

BERWYN COASTERS, LTD.

JERSEY

FUNNEL:

HOUSEFLAG:

SERVICES:

Berwyn Accord	...	...	...	1935	310	145	25	—	M(A)
Berwyn Baron	...	...	...	1936	311	135	25	11	M(A)

BLUE CIRCLE SHIPPING CO. LTD.

LONDON

FUNNEL: *Black with white band bordered by two blue bands in turn bordered by two yellow bands, with 'Blue' on the upper and 'Circle' on the lower.*

HOUSEFLAG: *As funnel bands.*

Walcrete	...	...	...	...	1949	1,364	235	36	10	SR(A)

Under 200 tons: **Ferrocrete** (1927/158 tons)

BLUE STAR LINE
(MANAGERS: GILLIE & BLAIR)

LONDON

FUNNEL: *Blue star on white disc on red with black top divided by white over black bands.*

HOUSEFLAG: *Red swallowtail pennant with blue star on white disc.*

Orwell	...	...	...	...	1956	495	173	28	11½	M(A)
Waveney	...	...	...	...	1956	499	169	27	—	M(A)

BOWKER & KING, LTD.

LONDON

FUNNEL: *Black with houseflag.*

HOUSEFLAG: *Quartered diagonally white over and under blue, with white diamond bearing the blue letters "B K" superimposed.*

SERVICES: *Thames tankers.*

Coastal Tankers:

Baccarat	...	...	...	...	1959	293	150	29	—	M(A)
Bannister	...	...	...	...	1944	227	143	21	—	M(A)
Batsman	...	...	...	...	1963	215	115	25	—	M(A)
Beefeater	...	...	...	...	1963	350	150	29	—	M(A)

Beresford	...	...	...	...	1959	304	138	27	—	M(A)
Black Knight	...	...	...	...	1960	481	169	34	—	M(A)
Bold Knight	...	...	...	...	1960	464	169	34	—	M(A)
Bowler	...	...	...	...	1963	210	135	28	—	M(A)
Burgundy	...	...	...	...	1962	323	135	28	—	M(A)
Busby	...	...	...	...	1963	200	115	25	—	M(A)

Under 200 tons: **Badger** (1915/139 tons), **Bradfield** (1917/136 tons) and **Brandram** (1915/158 tons)

R. S. BRIGGS (DON SHIPPING CO. LTD.)

LONDON

FUNNEL: *Black with broad red band.*

HOUSEFLAG:

Basildon	...	...	...	...	1945	1,058	212	33	10	SR(A)

BRISTOL STEAM NAVIGATION CO. LTD.

BRISTOL

FUNNEL: *Black or yellow with houseflag.*

HOUSEFLAG: *White with red St. Andrews Cross and blue letters "B S N C" in each quarter.*

SERVICES: *Bristol to Dublin, Antwerp and Rotterdam, calling at South Wales ports.*

Apollo	...	...	...	...	1954	1,266	255	39	12½	M(A)
Dido	...	...	...	...	1963	1,589	261	40	12½	M(A)
Echo	...	...	...	...	1954	1,266	255	39	12½	M(A)
Hero	...	...	...	...	1963	1,589	261	40	12½	M(A)
Juno	...	...	...	...	1949	969	224	33	11	M(A)
Milo	...	...	...	...	1953	991	224	34	11½	M(A)
Pluto	...	...	...	...	1950	988	224	33	11	M(A)
Sappho	...	...	...	...	1949	1,134	217	33	—	M(A)

BRITAIN STEAMSHIP CO. LTD.

LONDON

FUNNEL: *Black.*

HOUSEFLAG:

Balmoral Queen	...	...	...	1954	1,423	248	37	—	M(A)
Osborne Queen	...	...	...	1957	1,424	240	36	11½	M(A)
Richmond Queen	...	...	...	1958	1,326	235	36	12	M(A)
Sandringham Queen	...	...	1955	1,308	233	36	11	M(A)
Windsor Queen	...	...	...	1956	1,036	218	34	11	M(A)

M.V. Dover. British Rail. [*John G. Callis*

M.V. Apollo. Bristol S.N. Co. [*Fotoship*

BRITISH & CONTINENTAL STEAMSHIP CO. LTD.

LIVERPOOL

FUNNEL: *White with black top.*

HOUSEFLAG: *White swallowtail with red St. George's Cross and blue letters "B C S C" in each quarter.*

SERVICES: *Liverpool, Garston, Manchester and Ellesmere Port to Amsterdam, Rotterdam, Antwerp, Ghent, Dunkirk, etc. Belfast to Ghent and Terneuzen. Glasgow to Antwerp, Ghent and Terneuzen. (All cargo only).*

Bittern	...	...	...	...	1949	1,542	289	43	13	SR
Egret ...	...	...	...	...	1959	1,187	249	40	13	M(A)

BRITISH CHANNEL ISLANDS SHIPPING CO. LTD.
(COAST LINES GROUP)
LONDON

FUNNEL: *Yellow with black top separated by narrow blue band.*

HOUSEFLAG: *Quartered, blue and white over white and blue.*

SERVICES: *London–Channel Islands (Cargo).*

Alderney Coast	...	...	...	1940	567	176	28	11	M(A)
Devon Coast...	...	...	...	1937	972	—	—	—	—
Jersey Coast	...	...	...	1940	697	210	33	11	M(A)
Sark Coast ...	...	...	...	1937	646	209	35	10	M(A)
Southern Coast	...	...	...	1943	869	243	35	11	M(A)

BRITISH TRANSPORT COMMISSION (BRITISH RAILWAYS)

FUNNEL: *Red with black top and white British Rail "twin-arrow" device.*

HOUSEFLAG: *Blue with white "twin-arrow" device.*

These vessels are being repainted with blue hulls.

EASTERN REGION

SERVICES: *Harwich–Hook of Holland (Passenger). Harwich–Antwerp and Harwich–Rotterdam (Cargo, with limited passenger accommodation). Harwich–Zeebrugge (Train Ferry). Hull–New Holland (Passenger and Vehicle Ferry). Gravesend–Tilbury (Passenger Ferry).*

Amsterdam ...	...	...	...	1950	5,092	377	52	21½	ST(2)
Arnhem	...	...	...	1947	4,891	377	52	21	ST(2)
Avalon	...	...	...	1963	6,584	404	60	22	ST(2)
Colchester	...	...	...	1959	866	242	38	13½	M(A)
Isle of Ely	...	...	...	1958	866	242	38	13½	M(A)

M.V. Bardic Ferry. Atlantic S.N. Co.   [*J. Clarkson*

S.S. Twickenham Ferry. Angleterre-Lorraine-Alsace S.A. de Nav.
                    [*John G. Callis*

Train Ferries:

Cambridge Ferry	...	...	...	1963	3,294	403	61	14	M(2)
Essex Ferry	...	...	...	1957	3,242	400	61	13½	M(2)
Norfolk Ferry	...	...	...	1951	3,137	400	59	13	M(2)
Suffolk Ferry	...	...	...	1947	3,134	400	59	14	M(2)

Humber Ferries: (These vessels are operated by Associated Humber Lines and wear that company's funnel colours)

Lincoln Castle	...	...	...	1940	598	209	33	13½	SR(PW)
Tattershall Castle	...	...	...	1934	556	209	33	13½	SR(PW)
Wingfield Castle	...	...	...	1934	556	209	33	13½	SR(PW)

Under 200 tons: **Catherine, Edith** and **Rose** (All 1960)

LONDON MIDLAND REGION

SERVICES: *Holyhead–Dun Laoghaire (Passenger and Car Ferry); Heysham–Belfast (Passenger); Lake Windermere (Excursions); Holyhead–Dublin, Heysham–Belfast, Fishguard–Waterford (Cargo and/or Container Services).*

Cambria	...	...	...	...	1949	5,284	396	54	21	M(2)
Container Enterprise		...	...	...	1958	982	263	40	12½	M(A)
Container Venturer		...	...	...	1958	982	263	42	12½	M(A)
Duke of Argyll	...	...	...	...	1956	4,797	375	55	21	ST(2)
Duke of Lancaster	...	...	...	1956	4,797	375	55	21	ST(2)
Duke of Rothesay	...	...	...	1957	4,780	375	55	21	ST(2)
Great Western	...	...	...	...	1934	1,742	298	40	14	SR(2)
Hibernia	...	...	...	...	1949	4,972	396	54	21	M(2)
Holyhead Ferry	...	...	...	1965	3,800	369	57	—	M(2)
Selby	...	...	...	...	1959	963	232	39	12½	M(A)
Slieve Bawn	...	...	...	...	1936	1,447	310	45	17	ST(2)
Slieve Bearnagh	...	...	...	1936	1,451	310	45	17	ST(2)
Slieve Donard	...	...	...	...	1960	1,598	310	45	14	M(2)
Slieve League	...	...	...	...	1935	1,342	310	45	17	ST(2)
Harrogate	...	...	...	...	1959	963	232	39	12½	M(A)

Lake Windermere Excursions:

Swan	...	...	...	...	...	1938	251	142	25	11	M
Swift	...	...	...	...	...	1900	203	158	21	12	M
Teal	...	...	...	...	...	1936	251	142	25	11	M
Tern	...	...	...	...	...	1891	120	146	18	11	SR

SOUTHERN REGION

SERVICES: *Dover–Calais, Dover–Boulogne, Newhaven–Dieppe (Passenger and Car Ferry); Folkestone–Calais, Folkestone–Boulogne, Weymouth–Channel Islands (Passenger and Cargo); Southampton–Channel Islands (Cargo); Dover–Dunkirk (Train Ferry).*

Isle of Wight: Portsmouth–Ryde, Southsea–Ryde (Passenger); Portsmouth–Fishbourne, Lymington–Yarmouth (Car Ferry). Also Excursions from Portsmouth and Southsea. Certain of these services are operated only during the summer.

Caesaria	...	...	...	...	1960	4,174	322	54	20	ST(2)
Dover*	...	...	...	...	1965					
Elk	...	...	...	...	1959	795	228	40	14	M(2A)
Invicta	...	...	...	...	1940	4,191	348	50	22	ST(2)
Lord Warden *	...	...	...	1952	3,333	362	59	20	ST(2)
Maid of Kent*	...	...	...	1959	3,920	373	59	20½	ST(2)
Maid of Orleans	...	...	...	1949	3,777	341	50	22	ST(2)

Name				Year	Tonnage				Type
Moose	...	...	...	1959	795	228	32	14	M(2A)
Normannia*		...	...	1952	2,219	309	48	19½	ST(2)
St. Patrick	...	...	...	1948	3,482	321	48	20	ST(2)
Sarnia	...	...	...	1961	4,174	322	53	20	ST(2)
Winchester	...	...	...	1947	1,149	252	36	15	M(2)

Train Ferries:

Name				Year	Tonnage				Type
Hampton Ferry	...	...	...	1934	2,989	360	61	16½	ST(2)
Shepperton Ferry	...	...	...	1935	2,996	360	61	16½	ST(2)

Owned by French National Railways (S.N.C.F.) but working integrated services with Southern Region.

Name				Year	Tonnage				Type
Compiegne (F)*	...	...	...	1958	3,483	377	60	20	M(2)
Cote d'Azur (F)	...	...	...	1951	4,037	365	43	25½	ST(2)

Train Ferry:

Name				Year	Tonnage				Type
Saint-Germain (F)	...	...	...	1951	3,094	380	61	18½	M(2)

Owned by Angleterre-Lorraine-Alsace S.A. de Nav. but working as above (Funnel has white letters "ALA" instead of twin-arrow).

Train Ferry:

Name				Year	Tonnage				Type
Twickenham Ferry (F)	...	...	1934	2,839	360	61	16½	ST(2)

Jointly owned by B.T.C. and S.N.C.F. for Dieppe services. (Funnel: Yellow with black top)

Name				Year	Tonnage				Type
Brest (F)	...	...	...	1950	1,059	238	35	14	M(A)
Brighton	...	...	...	1950	2,875	311	41	24	ST(2)
Falaise*	...	...	...	1947	2,416	311	48	20½	ST(2)
Nantes (F)	...	...	...	1946	1,053	238	35	14	M(A)
Rennes (F)	...	...	...	1948	1,053	238	35	14	M(A)
Valencay (F)*	...	...	...	1965	3,477	344	56		M(2)
Villandry (F)*	...	...	...	1965	3,445	344	58		M(2)

Isle of Wight Ferries:

Name				Year	Tonnage				Type
Brading	...	...	...	1948	887	200	46	14½	M(2)
Camber Queen*	...	...	...	1961	293	166	43	10½	M(2)
Farringford*	...	...	...	1947	489	178	28	10½	ME(PW)
Lymington*	...	...	...	1938	275	148	37	9	M
Ryde	...	...	...	1937	566	223	29	14½	SR(PW)
Sandown	...	...	...	1934	684	223	29	14½	SR(PW)
Shanklin	...	...	...	1951	833	200	46	14½	M(2)
Southsea	...	...	...	1948	837	200	46	14½	M(2)

WESTERN REGION

SERVICES: *Kingswear–Dartmouth Ferry.*

Under 200 tons: **Adrian Gilbert** (1957/35 tons), **Humphrey Gilbert** 1957/35 tons.

FISHGUARD & ROSSLARE RAILWAYS & HARBOURS CO.

Owned jointly by the British Transport Commission and the Irish Transport Board (Coras Iompair Eireann).

FUNNEL: *Red with black top and white letters "F & R".*

SERVICES: *Fishguard–Rosslare (Passenger and Car ferry).*

Name				Year	Tonnage				Type
St. Andrew*	...	...	...	1932	3,035	338	47	21	ST(2)
St. David*	...	...	...	1947	3,352	321	48	20¾	ST(2)

*Car Ferries

S.S. Clangula. Built 1954. Bristol & Continental S.S. Co. (Since sold) [*Fotoship*

M.V. Southsea. British Rail.   [*John G. Callis*

BURNS & LAIRD LINES LTD.
(COAST LINES GROUP)
GLASGOW

FUNNEL: *Red with black top separated by narrow blue band.*

HOUSEFLAG: *Blue with yellow rampant lion and globe.*

SERVICES: *Glasgow–Belfast (Passenger); Ardrossan–Belfast (Passenger, summer only); Greenock/Glasgow to Belfast, Dublin and Londonderry (Cargo, with limited passenger accommodation); Liverpool–Sligo Cargo).*

Lairds Loch	...	...	...	...	1944	1,736	275	41	13	M(2)
Lairdsburn	...	...	...	...	1936	513	172	27	9	M(A)
Lairdscrest	...	...	...	...	1936	789	237	37	13½	M(2)
Lairdsglen	...	...	...	...	1954	1,543	298	43	14	M(2)
Lairdsrock	...	...	...	...	1935	471	171	27	9	M(A)
Royal Scotsman	...	...	...	1936	3,288	340	48	17	M(2)
Royal Ulsterman	...	...	...	1936	3,290	340	48	17	M(2)
Scottish Coast	...	...	...	1957	3,817	342	53	17	M(2)

CALEDONIAN STEAM PACKET CO. LTD.
(BRITISH TRANSPORT COMMISSION)
GLASGOW

FUNNEL: *Yellow with black top and red Scottish lion device.*

HOUSEFLAG:

SERVICES: *A network of Clyde services from Gourock, Craigendoran or Glasgow to Wemyss Bay, Largs and Fairlie with calls at Kilcreggan, Dunoon, Innellan, Rothesay and small ports. Summer extensions to (a) Tighnabruaich (Kyles of Bute). Brodick and Whiting Bay (Arran), (b) Tighnabruaich, Ardrishaig and Inverary (Loch Fyne), (c) Blairmore, Lochgoilhead, and Arrochar (Loch Long), (d) Millport (Cumbrae) and Lochranza (Arran), (e) Millport and Ayr. Fairlie to Millport (Cumbrae) and Kilchattan Bay (Bute). Ardrosan to Brodick and Whiting Bay. Summer excursions to the Lochs and round the Isles of the Firth of Clyde (Arran, Bute, the Cumbraes and Ailsa Craig). The boundaries of the area are Glasgow, Ayr, Ailsa Craig, Campbeltown, Ardrishaig, Inverary, Kyles of Bute, Lochgoilhead, Arrochar, Glasgow. Ferries: Gourock to Dunoon (car). Wemyss Bay to Rothesay (car). Largs to Millport. Loch Lomond, Ardlui to Balloch (summer only).*

Arran*	...	...	...	...	1953	568	186	35	15½	M(2)
Bute*	...	...	...	...	1954	570	186	36	15½	M(2)
Caledonia	...	...	...	...	1934	623	230	30	16¾	SR(PW)
Countess of Breadalbane			...	1936	106	93	18	10	M(2)
Cowal*	...	...	...	...	1954	569	186	35	15½	M(2)
Duchess of Hamilton		...	...	1932	801	272	32	20¼	ST(3)
Glen Sannox*	...	...	...	1957	1,107	257	44	17	M(2)
Maid of Argyll	...	...	...	1953	508	165	28	15	M(2)

[John G. Callis

S.S. St. Patrick. British Rail.

Maid of Ashton	...	...	...	1953	508	165	28	15	M(2)
Maid of Cumbrae	...	...	...	1953	508	165	28	15	M(2)
Maid of Skelmorlie	...	...	1953	508	165	28	15	M(2)
Queen Mary II	...	...	...	1933	1,014	263	35	19	ST(3)
Talisman	...	...	...	1935	544	223	28	17	ME(PW)
Waverley	...	...	...	1947	396	248	30	17	SR(PW)
Loch Lomond Services								
Maid of the Loch	...	...	...	1953	555	191	28	14	SR(PW)

Under 200 tons: Skye Ferries; **Broadford** (1954/57 tons), **Kyleakin** (1960/64 tons), **Lochalsh** (1957/64 tons) and **Portree** (1951/53 tons)

*Car Ferries

CALEDONIAN STEAM PACKET CO. (IRISH SERVICES) LTD.

SERVICES: *Stranraer–Larne (Passenger and Car Ferry).*

Caledonian Princess*	...	...	1961	3,629	353	57	20½	ST(2)

P. & A. CAMPBELL, LTD.

CARDIFF

FUNNEL: *White.*

HOUSEFLAG: *Blue pennant with white disc and chevron.*

SERVICES: *Passenger excursion services from Bristol, Weston-super-Mare, Newport, Cardiff, etc. to Swansea, Minehead, Lynmouth, Ilfracombe, and other Bristol Channel towns.*

Bristol Queen	...	...	...	1946	961	258	31	16½	SR(PW)
Cardiff Queen	...	...	...	1947	765	248	30	16½	SR(PW)
St. Trillo	...	...	...	1936	314	156	27	13½	M(2)

JOHN CARTER (POOLE) LTD.

POOLE

FUNNEL: *Yellow with narrow black top and black "C" in black bordered white diamond on red panel.*

HOUSEFLAG: *Red with black "C" in black bordered white diamond.*

Cranborne	...	...	...	1958	439	166	27	10	M(A)
Sherborne	...	...	...	1950	465	165	27	9½	M(A)
Wimborne	...	...	...	1949	368	147	25	9	M(A)

M.V. Duke of Lancaster still wearing old funnel colours. British Rail.

[*J. Clarkson*

M.V. Sherborne wearing Blue Star Line funnel colours. John Carter (Poole) Ltd.

[*A. Duncan*

CENTRAL ELECTRICITY GENERATING BOARD

LONDON

FUNNEL: *Red with black top and rings.*

HOUSEFLAG: *Divided vertically red, black and yellow, with red and yellow rampant lion device on the black.*

Barford	...	...	...	...	1950	3,357	339	46	10½	SR(A)
Battersea*	...	...	...	...	1951	1,777	271	40	11	M(A)
Blackwall Point*	...	...	...	1951	1,776	271	40	11	M(A)
Brimsdown*	...	...	...	1951	1,837	271	40	10	SR(A)
Brunswick Wharf*	...	...	...	1951	1,782	271	40	10	SR(A)
Capt. J. M. Donaldson	...	...	1951	3,357	339	46	10	SR(A)
Charles H. Merz	...	...	...	1955	2,947	340	43	11	SR(A)
Charles Parsons*	...	...	...	1936	1,539	247	39	9	SR(A)
Cliff Quay	...	...	...	...	1950	3,357	339	46	10½	SR(A)
Dame Caroline Haslett*		...	...	1950	1,777	271	39	11	M(A)
Deptford*	...	...	...	...	1951	1,782	271	40	10	M(A)
Fulham VIII*	...	...	...	1947	1,773	270	40	11	M(A)
Fulham IX*	...	...	...	1948	1,759	270	40	11	M(A)
Fulham X*	...	...	...	1948	1,759	270	40	11	M(A)
Hackney*	...	...	...	...	1952	1,782	271	40	10	SR(A)
Harry Richardson*	...	...	1930	1,777	271	39	11	M(A)
James Rowan	...	...	...	1955	2,947	340	44	11	SR(A)
Lord Citrine	...	...	...	1950	3,357	339	46	10½	SR(A)
Mendip	...	...	...	...	1950	1,362	235	36	10	SR(A)
Oliver Bury	...	...	...	1946	2,904	326	45	10	SR(A)
Pompey Light	...	...	...	1949	1,428	252	37	10	SR(A)
Sir Alexander Kennedy*	...	1946	1,714	271	40	9	SR(A)
Sir Archibald Page	...	...	1950	3,357	339	46	10	SR(A)
Sir John Snell	...	...	...	1955	2,947	340	47	11	SR(A)
Sir Johnstone Wright	...	...	1955	2,947	340	47	11	SR(A)
Sir Joseph Swan*	...	...	...	1945	1,554	257	40	10	SR(A)
Sir Leonard Pearce*	...	...	1941	1,580	257	40	9	SR(A)
Sir William Walker	...	...	1954	3,050	340	44	11¼	SR(A)
W. J. H. Wood	...	...	...	1951	3,357	339	46	10	SR(A)

*Up-river collier or "Flatiron"

Diesel Hopper Barges: **Bessie Surtees, Bobbie Shaftoe, Hexhamshire Lass** (All 620 tons), **Sir Fon** (1950/814 tons)

CHANNEL SHIPPING LTD.

JERSEY

FUNNEL:

HOUSEFLAG:

Concorde	...	...	...	...	1957	452	165	26	—	M(A)
Gorey	...	...	...	...	1949	427	161	24	10	M(A)
Grouville	...	...	...	...	1947	393	161	25	10	M(A)

WESTERN SHIPPING LTD.

Meledor	...	...	...	...	1951	485	167	28	—	M(A)
Treviscoe	...	...	...	...	1952	494	172	28	9	M(A)

S.S. Cliff Quay. Central Electricity Generating Board. [*John G. Callis*

M.V. Concorde. Channel Shpg. Co. [*John G. Callis*

CHARRINGTON GARDNER LOCKET (LONDON) LTD.

LONDON

FUNNEL: *Yellow with black top and broad blue band between two white rings.*

HOUSEFLAG: *Blue pennant with blue "C" on white disc joined to points of flag by white stripes.*

Lady Charrington	1952	2,154	285	41	10	SR(A)
Coastal Tankers (Thames services):						
Charcrest	1964	480	163	32	—	M(A)
Charmo	1960	477	163	33	—	M(A)

CLYDE SHIPPING CO. LTD.

GLASGOW

FUNNEL: *Black.*

HOUSEFLAG: *Blue pennant with white lighthouse and white letters "C S C".*

SERVICES: *Liverpool–Waterford (Cargo), Preston–Waterford (Containers).*

Tuskar	1962	1,115	272	43	14	M

Also a large fleet of tugs operating from Glasgow and Greenock

COAST LINES LTD.

LIVERPOOL

FUNNEL: *Black with white chevron.*

HOUSEFLAG: *Blue, white, red, white, blue, horizontal stripes with blue letters "C L" superimposed.*

SERVICES: *Liverpool–Plymouth–Southampton–London, London–Cork–Dublin, and London–Belfast. (Cargo, but with passenger accommodation in summer).*

Adriatic Coast	1949	1,050	247	38	12	M(A)
Caledonian Coast	1948	1,265	277	40	14	M(A)
Cambrian Coast	1958	560	187	30	10	M(A)
Cheshire Coast	1954	1,202	256	39	12	M(A)
Dorset Coast	1959	1,125	220	36	11½	M(A)
Hibernian Coast	1947	1,258	277	40	14	M(A)
Irish Coast	1952	3,824	340	52	17½	M(2)
Kentish Coast	1946	498	201	30	12	M(A)
Lancashire Coast	1954	1,283	256	38	12	M(A)
Mersey Coast	1939	509	202	32	10	M(A)
Pacific Coast	1947	1,188	266	38	12	M(2A)
Wirral Coast	1962	881	203	36	12	M(A)

M.V. Caledonian Coast. Coast Lines Ltd. [*Fotoship*

M.V. Cabourne. Coastal Carriers Ltd. [*D. R. Chesterton*

COASTAL CARRIERS LTD.
NEWCASTLE

FUNNEL: *Red with houseflag.*

HOUSEFLAG: *Quartered diagonally white above and below blue, with red "C C" in white quarters.*

Cabourne	...	...	...	...	1931	528	165	26	—	M(A)

COASTAL STEAM PACKET CO. LTD.
LONDON

FUNNEL: *Red with black top separated by narrow white band.*

HOUSEFLAG:

COASTAL EXCURSIONS:

Queen of the South	...	...	1931	839	258	58	—	ME(PW)

S. W. COE & CO. LTD.
LIVERPOOL

FUNNEL: *Yellow with black top separated by white over red bands.*

HOUSEFLAG:

These vessels have pale green hulls.

SERVICES: *Liverpool–Coleraine (Cargo).*

Blackthorn	...	...	...	...	1960	749	190	34	—	M(A)
Maythorn	...	...	...	...	1962	779	190	34	—	M(A)
Silverthorn	...	...	...	...	1958	500	180	29	—	M(A)

COLCHESTER SHIPPING CO. LTD.
LONDON

FUNNEL:

HOUSEFLAG:

Eldorita	...	...	...	...	1920	201	109	22	—	SR(A)

COMMODORE SHIPPING CO. LTD.
GUERNSEY

FUNNEL:

HOUSEFLAG:

SERVICES: *Guernsey–Alderney and Sark (Passenger). Portsmouth–Channel Islands, Rainham, Kent–Channel Islands (Cargo).*

Commodore Queen	...	...	1944	309	160	25	—	M(A)

Under 200 tons: **Fleet Commodore** (—/95 tons), **Island Commodore** (1941/195 tons)

CONSTANTINE SHIPPING CO. LTD.

MIDDLESBROUGH

FUNNEL: *Red with black top and one black band.*

HOUSEFLAG: *White with red St. George's Cross broken at centre by red bordered white disc containing black letter "C".*

Copsewood	...	...	...	...	1951	1,272	226	36	10	M(A)
Eastwood	...	...	...	...	1960	1,753	271	39	11½	M(A)
Eskwood	...	...	...	...	1951	1,273	226	36	10	M(A)
Thameswood	...	...	...	...	1957	1,799	271	39	11½	M(A)
Tynewood	...	...	...	...	1957	1,495	237	38	10½	M

COPPACK BROS. & CO.

CONNAHS QUAY

FUNNEL: *Yellow with black top.*

HOUSEFLAG:

Indorita	...	...	...	...	1920	201	115	22	9	M(A)

COQUET SHIPPING CO.
(ANTHONY & BAINBRIDGE, LTD.)

NEWCASTLE

FUNNEL:

HOUSEFLAG:

Gracechurch	...	...	...	1952	942	214	33	10	M(A)

CORY MARITIME LTD.

LONDON

FUNNEL: *Black with black diamond on broad white band.*

HOUSEFLAG: *Red with large white diamond.*

Corbank	...	...	...	...	1956	2,106	277	39	12	M(A)
Corbeach	...	...	...	...	1957	2,106	277	39	12	M(A)
Corbrae	...	...	...	...	1952	2,002	272	39	10	M(A)
Corburn	...	...	...	...	1953	2,059	279	39	10	M(A)
Corchester	...	...	...	...	Bldg.	4,800	370	53	—	M(A)
Corfoss	...	...	...	...	1942	1,849	265	39	9½	SR(A)
Cormain	...	...	...	...	1942	2,883	326	44	10	SR(A)
Cormist	...	...	...	...	1946	2,885	326	44	10	SR(A)
Cormount	...	...	...	...	1944	2,871	329	44	10	SR(A)

24

M.V. Eastwood. Constantine Shpg. Co. *[Fotoship*

M.V. Corbrae. Wm. Cory & Son. *[Fotoship*

Corsea	...	...	...	...	1957	3,373	339	46	10	M(A)
Corsound	...	...	...	...	1953	3,374	339	46	9¾	SR(A)
Corstar	...	...	...	...	1956	3,379	339	46	10	M(A)
Corstream	...	...	...	...	1955	3,375	339	46	9¾	SR(A)

Coastal Tankers: (Late Bulk Oil Co.)

Pass of Balmaha	...	...	...	1942	784	202	31	9	SR(A)
Pass of Dalveen	...	...	...	1958	965	217	31	11½	M(A)
Pass of Glenclunie ...	...	...	1963	1,416	245	37	11½	M(A)
Pass of Glenogle	...	...	...	1963	860	203	33	11½	M(A)
Pass of Kildrummy	...	...	1959	965	217	32	11½	M(A)
Pass of Melfort	...	...	...	1961	970	211	34	11	M(A)

Thames Tankers: (Cory Tank Lighterage, Ltd.)

Bruce Stone ...	...	...	...	1964	357	143	30	—	M(A)
London Stone	...	...	...	1957	438	155	31	—	M(A)

Under 200 tons: **Rebus Stone** (1963/177 tons), **Rufus Stone** (1963/165 tons). Also Ocean Freighters

COSENS & CO. LTD.

WEYMOUTH

FUNNEL: *Yellow with black top.*

HOUSEFLAG:

SERVICES: *Coastal excursion services from Weymouth and Swanage.*

Embassy	...	...	...	...	1911	446	190	26	13½	SR(PW)

HUGH CRAIG & CO. LTD.

BELFAST

FUNNEL: *Yellow with black top separated by broad red band.*

HOUSEFLAG: *White with blue border at top and bottom and a red "C" surrounding a small blue disc at centre.*

SERVICES: *Belfast–Preston (Cargo).*

Craigmore	...	...	...	...	1965	1,350	239	37	—	M(A)

R. CUNNINGHAM

BELFAST

FUNNEL:

HOUSEFLAG:

Glas Island	...	...	...	...	1935	211	104	24	9	M(A)
Isle of Harris	...	...	...	1934	268	121*	22	10	M(A)
Isle of Lewis	...	...	...	1959	365	144	25	10	M(A)

M.V. Isle of Lewis. R. Cunningham.   [*J. Clarkson*

M.V. Mayfair Sapphire. A. S. Davidson Ltd.   [*J. Clarkson*

CURRIE LINE LTD.

EDINBURGH

FUNNEL: *Black with broad white band.*

HOUSEFLAG: *Blue swallowtail pennant with red border at top and bottom and a white "X" over a white cross in the hoist.*

SERVICES: *Leith–Copenhagen, Leith and Grangemouth–Hamburg and Bremen (Passenger and Cargo). Liverpool and Manchester–Hamburg and Bremen, Grangemouth and Middlesbrough–Finnish ports, and London–Lisbon and Mediterranean ports (Cargo).*

Courland	...	...	...	...	1956	877	222	36	11½	M(A)
England	...	...	...	...	1947	2,271	334	46	12	M
Finland	...	...	...	...	1956	877	225	36	11½	M(A)
Ireland	...	...	...	...	1951	2,508	342	46	14	M
Pentland	...	...	...	...	1958	880	225	36	12	M(A)
Scotland	...	...	...	...	1946	2,271	334	46	12	M
Zealand	...	...	...	...	1955	2,030	270	45	12½	M

Also larger Ocean Freighters

A. S. DAVIDSON LTD.

BELFAST

FUNNEL: *Red with black top separated by broad yellow and narrow blue bands.*

HOUSEFLAG:

Mayfair Sapphire	...	...	...	1949	1,032	214	34	10½	M(A)

J. A. DAVIDSON LTD.

ABERDEEN

FUNNEL:

HOUSEFLAG:

Torquay	...	...	...	...	1963	443	167	27	—	M(A)

ONESIMUS DOREY & SONS, LTD.

GUERNSEY

FUNNEL: *Black with blue "D" on white diamond interrupting blue band.*

HOUSEFLAG: *Red with blue "D" on large white diamond.*

Havelet	...	...	...	...	1964	1,043	217	34	10	M(A)
Portelet	...	...	...	...	1962	1,043	217	34	10	M(A)

DUNDEE, PERTH & LONDON SHIPPING CO. LTD.

DUNDEE

FUNNEL: *Red with black top.*

HOUSEFLAG: *Red with white St. George's cross and white letters "D P L C" in each quarter, in the centre a white "&" in a small blue square.*

Dundee	...	...	...	...	1954	1,781	259	43	11½	M(A)
Lochee	...	...	...	...	1941	872	211	33	10	M(A)
Coastal Tanker:									
Kingennie	...	...	...	...	1958	1,168	231	36	11½	M(A)

LOCKETT WILSON LINE, LTD.

Vauban	...	...	...	...	1963	370	148	24	—	M(A)
Vendome	...	...	...	...	1963	369	148	24	—	M(A)

EAST ANGLIAN SHIPPING CO. LTD.

LOWESTOFT

FUNNEL: *Grey with houseflag.*

HOUSEFLAG: *Blue with white crown and red roses.*

SERVICES: *Lowestoft–Rotterdam (Cargo)*

Under 200 tons: **Yarvic** (1944/149 tons)

ELLERMAN'S WILSON LINE LTD.

HULL

FUNNEL: *Red with black top.*

HOUSEFLAG: *White swallowtail pennant with a red disc in the hoist. Flown under blue pennant bearing the white letters "JRE".*

The vessels have green hulls.

SERVICES: *Hull–Oslo, Hull–Copenhagan. Hull–Gothenburg, Hull–Stockholm London to the above ports and to Gdynia. Liverpool and Manchester–Stockholm (Passenger and Cargo). Hull and Grimsby to Norwegian ports, Liverpool, Manchester and Bristol Channel ports to Norway. Hull and Grimsby and/or Middlesbrough to Swedish ports. Liverpool and Manchester to Swedish ports (Cargo). Goole–Copenhagen.*

Aaro	...	...	...	...	1963	2,468	330	49	13½	M
Ariosto	...	...	...	...	1946	2,203	307	44	13½	RT
Borodino	...	...	...	...	1950	3,206	312	49	13½	RT
Bravo	...	...	...	...	1947	1,798	297	42	13½	RT
Byland Abbey		...	...	...	1957	1,372	265	40	13¼	M(A)
Carlo	...	...	...	...	1947	1,799	297	42	13½	RT
Cattaro	...	...	...	...	1945	2,890	356	48	13	SR

S.S. Livorno. Ellerman's Wilson Line. *[D. R. Chesterton*

M.V. Brodick. Enid Shpg Co. *[J. Clarkson*

Cicero	...	...	...	...	1954	2,497	310	49	13½	RT
Cavallo	...	...	...	...	1951	2,340	310	49	13	M
Electro	...	...	...	...	1937	793	199	29	10	M(A)
Kirkham Abbey	...	...	...	1956	1,372	265	40	13¼	M(A)
Leo	...	...	...	...	1947	1,792	297	42	13½	RT
Livorno	...	...	...	...	1946	2,957	356	50	13	SR
Malmo	...	...	...	...	1946	1,779	297	42	13½	RT
Rinaldo	...	...	...	...	1946	2,957	356	50	13	SR
Rollo	...	...	...	...	1954	2,499	310	49	13	RT
Salerno	...	...	...	...	1965	1,590	308	45	13½	M(A)
Silvio	...	...	...	...	1947	1,798	297	42	13¼	RT
Spero	...	...	...	...		Building				
Teano	...	...	...	...	1955	1,580	277	43	13	RT
Tinto	...	...	...	...	1947	1,795	297	42	13½	RT
Trentino	...	...	...	...	1952	2,340	310	49	13½	M
Truro	...	...	...	...	1947	1,795	297	42	13½	RT
Volo	...	...	...	...	1946	1,797	297	42	13½	RT

Also larger Ocean Freighters

ELLIS & McHARDY LTD.

ABERDEEN

FUNNEL: *Yellow with black top separated by an interlocking band of red triangles.*

HOUSEFLAG:

Spray ...	...	...	...	...	1963	900	195	33	—	M(A)

ELWICK BAY SHIPPING CO. LTD.

KIRKWALL

FUNNEL:

HOUSEFLAG:

SERVICES: *Generally confined to Scottish ports and Orkneys.*

Elwick Bay ...	...	...	...	1930	264	122	23	9½	M(A)

ENID SHIPPING CO. LTD.

LEITH

FUNNEL: *Yellow with narrow black top and houseflag.*

HOUSEFLAG: *Blue with white St. Andrews' Cross with red lion rampant superimposed.*

Brodick	...	...	...	...	1952	701	200*	27	—	M(A)
Hawick	...	...	...	...	1948	444	153	27	10	M(A)
Hillswick	...	...	...	...	1957	377	156	26	—	M(A)
Lerwick	...	...	...	...	1950	376	151	25	9½	M(A)

M.V. Esso Woolston. Esso Petroleum Co.　　　　　　　　[*John G. Callis*

M.V. Gillian Everard. P. T. Everard & Sons.　　　　　　　[*John G. Callis*

ESSO PETROLEUM CO. LTD.

LONDON

FUNNEL: *Black with red "Esso" in blue ring on broad white band.*

HOUSEFLAG: *Red "Esso" in blue ring on white field.*

Coastal Tankers:

Esso Brixham	...	...	...	1957	828	213	32	10	M(A)
Esso Caernarvon	...	...	...	1962	1,103	231	36	10	M(A)
Esso Chelsea...	...	...	...	1945	4,352	366	60	7½	SR(2A)
Esso Dover	...	...	...	1961	500	164	27	9½	M(A)
Esso Fulham	...	...	...	1945	4,352	366	60	7½	SR(2A)
Esso Hythe	...	...	...	1959	856	208	34	10	M(A)
Esso Ipswich	...	...	...	1960	1,103	231	36	10	M(A)
Esso Jersey	...	...	...	1962	300	121	24	—	M(A)
Esso Lyndhurst	...	...	...	1958	856	209	36	10	M(A)
Esso Ottawa...	...	...	...	1943	299	135	24	8	M(A)
Esso Poole	...	...	...	1955	754	196	34	9	M(A)
Esso Preston...	...	...	...	1956	2,500	299	42	10½	SR(A)
Esso Tynemouth	...	...	...	1960	528	171	28	9½	M(A)
Esso Woolston	...	...	...	1957	890	208	34	10	M(A)

F. T. EVERARD & SONS, LTD.

LONDON

FUNNEL: *Black with house flag, or yellow with houseflag. (Some vessels have pale blue or yellow hulls).*

HOUSEFLAG: *Divided diagonally white over red over white.*

Ability	...	...	...	...	1943	881	203	30	10	M(A)
Activity	...	...	...	...	1931	358	141	25	9	M(A)
Adaptity	...	...	...	...	1945	945	201	31	10	M(A)
Amenity	...	...	...	...	1944	881	202	30	10	M(A)
Angularity	...	...	...	...	1941	878	211	33	13	M(A)
Apricity	...	...	...	...	1933	402	149	26	10½	M(A)
Aridity	...	...	...	...	1931	336	136	24	9	M(A)
Aseity	...	...	...	...	1935	416	149	27	10½	M(A)
Atomicity	...	...	...	...	1947	592	184	28	10½	M(A)
Austerity	...	...	...	...	1947	592	184	28	10½	M(A)
Capacity	...	...	...	...	1963	461	170	28	—	M(A)
Celebrity	...	...	...	...	1947	324	145	25	9	M(A)
Centricity	...	...	...	...	1955	655	184	29	10	M(A)
Century	...	...	...	...	1956	780	204	30	10	M(A)
Clarity	...	...	...	...	1957	764	204	30	10	M(A)
Continuity	...	...	...	...	1955	655	184	29	10	M(A)
Ethel Everard	...	...	...	...	1957	1,542	231	38	10	M(A)
Fixity	...	...	...	...	Building					
Frederick T. Everard	...	...	...	1954	2,535	306	42	10	M(A)
Georgina V. Everard	...	...	...	1955	2,536	306	42	10	M(A)
Gillian Everard	...	...	...	1963	1,598	266	39	10	M(A)
Penelope Everard	...	...	...	1962	1,584	264	39	10	M(A)
Rosemary Everard	...	...	...	1965	1,598	266	39	10	M(A)
Sagacity	...	...	...	...	1946	943	211	31	10	M(A)
Sanguity	...	...	...	...	1956	1,577	241	38	10	M(A)
Scarcity	...	...	...	...	1948	586	184	28	10½	M(A)
Sedulity	...	...	...	...	1936	490	159	28	10½	M(A)
Selectivity	...	...	...	...	1952	1,575	241	38	10½	M(A)
Seniority	...	...	...	...	1951	1,566	243	38	10½	M(A)
Serenity	...	...	...	...	1941	557	176	28	11	M(A)
Seriality	...	...	...	...	1952	1,575	241	38	10½	M(A)
Severity	...	...	...	...	1954	590	184	28	10	M(A)

C

S.S. City. F. T. Everard & Sons.

[*D. R. Chesterton*

S.S. Authenticity. F. T. Everard & Sons.

[*J. Clarkson*

Signality	...	...	...	...	1937	487	165	28	10½	M(A)
Similarity	...	...	...	...	1951	1,575	241	38	10½	M(A)
Sincerity	...	...	...	...	1936	634	182	28	10½	M(A)
Singularity	...	...	...	...	1952	1,566	242	38	10¼	M(A)
Sociality	...	...	...	...	1953	500	187	29	10	M(A)
Sonority	...	...	...	...	1952	589	184	28	11	M(A)
Speciality	...	...	...	...	1951	1,570	241	38	10	M(A)
Spirality	...	...	...	...	1939	554	176	28	11	M(A)
Spontaneity		...	...	...	1949	499	169	28	11	M(A)
Suavity	...	...	...	...	1946	943	211	31	10	M(A)
Summity	...	...	...	...	1939	554	176	28	11	M(A)
Superiority	...	...	...	...	1947	2,145	283	41	10½	M(A)
William J. Everard		...	...	1963	1,589	266	39	10½	M(A)

Coastal Tankers:

Acclivity		...	...	...	1929	1,179	222	36	12	SR(A)
Acuity	...	...	...	...	1946	891	201	32	9½	M(A)
Adroity	...	...	...	...	1947	457	150	25	8½	M(A)
Agility	...	...	...	...	1959	1,016	214	35	12	M(A)
Alchymist	...	...	...	...	1945	813	202	31	9	SR(A)
Alignity	...	...	...	...	1945	890	201	32	9½	M(A)
Annuity	...	...	...	...	1961	1,599	266	40	10	M(A)
Anonity	...	...	...	...	1945	890	201	32	9	M(A)
Anteriority	...	...	...	...	1954	2,003	277	42	10	M(A)
Aptity	...	...	...	...	1939	434	167	26	9	M(A)
Arduity	...	...	...	...	1946	959	201	34	10½	M(A)
Argosity	...	...	...	...	1941	877	221	31	9½	SR(A)
Asperity	...	...	...	...	1942	667	184	31	9	M(A)
Assiduity	...	...	...	...	1964	1,249	234	36	10	M(A)
Assurity	...	...	...	...	1956	2,238	282	42	10	M(A)
Astrality	...	...	...	...	1945	3,744	358	48	12	M(A)
Atonality	...	...	...	...	1950	1,221	231	36	10	M(A)
Audacity	...	...	...	...	1943	656	177	31	10	M(A)
Aureity	...	...	...	...	1942	813	202	31	9	SR(A)
Auspicity	...	...	...	...	1944	402	148	27	8	M(A)
Austility	...	...	...	...	1946	933	202	34	9½	M(A)
Authenticity	...	...	...	...	1947	861	188	31	10	SR(A)
Averity	...	...	...	...	1944	401	148	27	8	M(A)
Awardity	...	...	...	...	1937	479	168	26	9½	M(A)
Candourity	...	...	...	...	1946	474	165	28	8½	SR(A)
City	...	...	...	...	1945	352	133	25	8	SR(A)
Clanity	...	...	...	...	1946	495	172	28	9	SR(A)
Commodity	...	...	...	...	1943	469	163	28	8	SR(A)
Conformity	...	...	...	...	1940	484	172	28	9	SR(A)
Grit	...	...	...	...	1958	2,739	310	45	10½	M(A)

Under 200 tons: **Attunity** (1945/149 tons), **Festivity** (1964/199 tons), **Frivolity** (1963/199 tons), **Tankity** (1945/145 tons), and **Totality** (1946/145 tons). **Cambria**—Sailing Barge (108 tons), **Will Everard**—Aux (188 tons)

JAMES FISHER & SON, LTD.
BARROW

FUNNEL: *Yellow with black top and black letter "F" on broad white band.*
HOUSEFLAG: *White with narrow red border and blue letter "F".*

Bay Fisher	...	...	...	...	1958	1,240	221	37	10½	M(A)
Eden Fisher		...	...	...	1965	1,200	233	35	11	M(A)
Firth Fisher		...	...	...	1950	974	220	33	10	M(A)
Leven Fisher	...	...	...	...	1962	1,541	260	39	11	M(A)
Pool Fisher	...	...	...	...	1959	1,028	218	34	11	M(A)
Race Fisher	...	...	...	...	1942	739	193	30	10½	M(A)
River Fisher	...	...	...	...	1941	733	192	30	11	M(A)
Stream Fisher		...	...	...	1943	745	192	30	10½	M(A)

M.V. Race Fisher. James Fisher & Son.   [*J. Clarkson*

M.V. Walnut. Jos. Fisher & Sons.   [*Fotoship*

SEAWAY COASTERS, LTD.								
Lune Fisher ...	...	...	...	1962	1,012	218	34	11	M(A)

LEO LINES LTD.							
Marchon Enterprise	...	...	1957	1,599	265	41	11	M(A)
Marchon Venturer	...	...	1962	1,599	261	39	11	M(A)

ASTORIA SHIPPING & TRANSPORTS, LTD.							
Marchon Trader	...	...	...	1957	1,915	265	41	11	M(A)

JOSEPH FISHER & SONS, LTD.

NEWRY

FUNNEL: *Black with red over white over blue band.*

HOUSEFLAG: *Divided diagonally from bottom of hoist, red over white over blue, with large black letter "F" on white stripe.*

Olive ...	...	...	...	...	1963	791	202	33	—	M(A)
Walnut	...	...	...	...	1955	539	185	28	—	M(A)

FLEETWOOD TANKERS, LTD.

FLEETWOOD

FUNNEL: *Red with black top.*

HOUSEFLAG:

Coastal Tankers:								
Onward Progress ...	...	...	1959	392	144	27	—	M(A)

Under 200 tons: **Onward Venture** (1962/175 tons)

Wm. FRANCE, FENWICK & CO. LTD.

LONDON

FUNNEL: *Black with red letters "F F" on broad white band.*

HOUSEFLAG: *Red with blue St. George's cross and white rectangle superimposed on centre.*

Bearwood	...	...	...	...	1955	3,393	344	46	10½	SR(A)
Birdwood	...	...	...	...	1945	2,862	329	45	9½	M(A)
Bushwood	...	...	...	...	1953	3,898	357	50	—	M(A)
Chelwood	...	...	...	...	1965	5,530	370	54	—	M(A)
Helmwood	...	...	...	...	1956	3,403	344	46	10½	SR(A)
Pinewood	...	...	...	...	1945	2,853	329	45	9½	SR(A)

Also larger Ocean Freighters.

S.S. Helmwood. Wm. France, Fenwick & Co.   [*A. Duncan*

M.V. Saint Blane. J. & A. Gardner & Co.   [*J. Clarkson*

38

J. & A. CARDNER, LTD.

GLASGOW

FUNNEL: *Black with white band.*

HOUSEFLAG: *Blue with large red letter "G".*

Saint Aidan	...	...	...	...	1963	980	218	34	12	M(A)
Saint Angus	...	...	...	...	1936	391	151	24	11	M(A)
Saint Blane	...	...	...	...	1955	650	199	29	12	M(A)
Saint Brandon	...	...	...	...	1960	699	196	30	12	M(A)
Saint Bridget	...	...	...	...	1953	709	190	32	10	M(A)
Saint Colman	...	...	...	...	1963	975	205	33	12	M(A)
Saint Modan	...	...	...	...	1960	488	166	27	11	M(A)
Saint Rule	...	...	...	...	1956	524	172	27	9	M(A)

GEM LINE, LTD.

(WM. ROBERTSON, SHIPOWNERS LTD.)

GLASGOW

FUNNEL: *Black.*

HOUSEFLAG: *Divided horizontally, blue, white and blue, with red "R" on white.*

Amber	...	...	...	...	1956	1,596	268	39	$12\frac{1}{2}$	M(A)
Amethyst	...	...	...	...	1958	1,548	258	40	12	M(A)
Brilliant	...	...	...	...	1958	1,143	224	34	11	M(A)
Cameo	...	...	...	...	1952	1,597	275	40	$10\frac{1}{2}$	M(A)
Emerald	...	...	...	...	1952	1,454	233	38	$10\frac{1}{2}$	M(A)
Jacinth	...	...	...	...	1937	650	185	28	$9\frac{1}{2}$	M(A)
Jade	...	...	...	...	1938	946	213	33	10	M(A)
Olivine	...	...	...	...	1952	1,354	245	38	$10\frac{1}{2}$	M(A)
Pearl	...	...	...	...	1953	1,093	212	34	$10\frac{1}{4}$	M(A)
Prase	...	...	...	...	1938	374	146	24	$9\frac{1}{2}$	M(A)
Spinel	...	...	...	...	1937	650	185	29	$9\frac{1}{2}$	M(A)
Topaz	...	...	...	...	1962	1,597	268	40	12	M(A)
Turquoise	...	...	...	...	1947	547	171	29	$9\frac{1}{2}$	M(A)
Tourmaline	...	...	...	...	1963	1,581	268	40	12	M(A)

GENERAL STEAM NAVIGATION CO. LTD.

LONDON

FUNNEL: *Black with houseflag. (Passenger excursion vessels: Yellow with houseflag).*

HOUSEFLAG: *White with red globe surmounting date "1824" in centre and red letters "G S N C" in each corner.*

SERVICES: *London (Tower Pier) to Gravesend, Southend, Margate and Ramsgate; Gravesend to Southend and Clacton; Gravesend and Southend to Calais, Boulogne, or Dunkirk. (Passenger excursions in summer) London to French ports; London to Hamburg, Bremen, and Rhine ports; London to Antwerp, Ghent, and sometimes Terneuzen; London to Amsterdam, Rotterdam, and Harlingen; London to Oporto; London, Newcastle, Middlesbrough to the Mediterranean; London to Hull and Grimsby; Bristol to Tonnay–Charente; Bristol Channel ports to Hamburg and Bremen; Southampton to Hamburg, Bremen, Antwerp, Rotterdam, Havre, Danish ports and Gothenburg. Shoreham to Bordeaux apd Tonnay–Charente; North French ports to the Mediterranean. (Cargo, with limited passenger accommodation in certain cases).*

Thames and English Channel Excursion Services:						
Queen of the Channel	1949	1,472	272	40	18½	M(2)
Royal Daffodil	1939	2,061	313	50	21	M(2)
Royal Sovereign	1948	1,851	288	49	20	M(2)
Cargo vessels:						
Adjutant	1954	1,366	260	40	13	M
Albatross	1965	654	213	36	13	M(A)
Alouette	1938	276	158	26	8½	M(A)
Auk	1949	1,238	259	40	12½	M(2)
Avocet	1965		Building			M(A)
Corncrake	1946	640	191	33	9½	M(A)
Drake	1938	531	193	31	10½	M
Gannet	1956	923	232	38	11½	M
Grebe	1948	933	235	37	11½	M
Greenfinch	1940	392	188	28	8	M(A)
Heron	1957	920	233	38	12	M
Hirondelle	1950	757	209	36	11½	M(A)
Kingfisher	1944	493	170	27	10	M(A)
Lapwing	1944	921	209	31	9½	M(A)
Marsworth	1952	628	188	30	—	M(A)
Mavis	1946	381	150	26	8	M(A)
Oriole	1964	430	149	28	12	M(A)
Ortolan	1964	430	149	28	12	M(A)
Peregrine	1941	890	211	33	10½	M(A)
Petrel	1965	450	160	29	—	M(A)
Philomel	1956	1,662	258	43	—	M(A)
Redstart	1946	640	191	33	9½	M(A)
Ringdove	1954	1,102	249	38	13	M
Sandpiper	1957	916	233	38	12	M
Seamew	1947	1,220	259	40	12	M(2)
Sheldrake	1956	1,662	258	43	—	M(A)
Stork	1946	493	170	27	9½	M(A)
Swallow	1947	1,413	280	41	10½	M
Swift	1950	757	209	36	11½	M(A)
Woodlark	1956	933	232	38	11½	M(A)
Woodwren	1954	968	219	38	12	M(A)

M.V. Lapwing. General Steam Navigation Co. [*Fotoship*

M.V. Shetland Trader. Hay & Co. (Lerwick) Ltd. [*John G. Callis*

M.V. Ringdove. General Steam Navigation Co.

GEORGE GIBSON & CO. LTD.

LEITH

FUNNEL: *Black, or with addition of crossed houseflags if working on Gibson–Rankine routes.*

HOUSEFLAG: *Divided horizontally, red over white over blue, with red letters "G G & Co" on white.*

SERVICES: *Aberdeen to Antwerp, North French ports, Lisbon and Oporto; Dundee to Rotterdam, Antwerp, Ghent, Amsterdam and North French ports; Grangemouth to Rotterdam, Antwerp, etc.; Leith to Antwerp, Rotterdam, Amsterdam, Ghent, Dunkirk, Rouen, Paris, Lisbon and Oporto; Middlesbrough to Antwerp, Dunkirk and Rouen.*

Bucklaw	...	...	...	...	1943	424	181	30	10½	M(A)
Cardrona	...	...	...	...	1947	1,526	260	37	10½	M(A)
Crichtoun		...	...	...	1946	873	211	33	11	M(A)
Dryburgh	...	...	...	...	1952	1,152	251	38	13	M(A)
Eildon	...	...	...	...	1936	1,640	262	37	10	M(A)
Ettrick	...	...	...	...	1959	1,144	261	39	13	M(A)
Heriot	...	...	...	...	1947	558	198	31	13	M(A)
Lanrick	...	...	...	...	1957	570	244	36	12½	M(A)
Melrose	...	...	...	...	1949	1,076	261	38	13	M(A)
Quentin	...	...	...	...	1940	500	174	28	10½	M(A)
Yarrow	...	...	...	...	1958	1,140	261	39	13	M(A)

G. T. GILLIE & BLAIR, LTD.

NEWCASTLE ON TYNE

FUNNEL: *Black with broad band between two narrow white bands.*

HOUSEFLAG: *Blue pennant with narrow white stripe near top and bottom.*

Arran Firth	...	...	...	1957	531	189	28	10½	M(A)
Moray Firth IV	...	...	...	1960	613	182	29	—	M(A)
Olna Firth	...	...	...	...	1957	591	177	29	10¾	M(A)
Pentland Firth	...	...	...	1955	594	177	29	10	M(A)

The company also manages the coasters Orwell and Waveney for the Blue Star Line, q.v.

GLEN & CO. LTD.

(SUBSIDIARY OF F. T. EVERARD & SONS, LTD., LONDON)

GLASGOW

FUNNEL: *Red with deep black top and with the Everard houseflag on the latter.*

HOUSEFLAG: *As for F. T. Everard & Sons.*

Stability	...	...	...	...	1949	1,490	242	36	11	M(A)
Winga	...	...	...	...	1957	2,234	298	44	—	SR

GREAT YARMOUTH SHIPPING CO. LTD.

GREAT YARMOUTH

FUNNEL: *Yellow with black top.*

HOUSEFLAG: *Quartered diagonnally, black over yellow over black, with the letters "G Y S Co" in each quarter, black on yellow and yellow on black.*

SERVICES: *Yarmouth and Kings Lynn to Boston and Antwerp; Yarmouth to Rotterdam; and Felixstowe to Amsterdam and Harlingen. All cargo only.*

Norfolk Trader	...	...	...	1954	457	164	28	—	M(A)
Norwich Trader	...	...	...	1944	377	150	26	8	M(A)

J. H. GRIFFIN

GREAT YARMOUTH

FUNNEL: *White with blue letter "G".*

HOUSEFLAG: *As Funnel.*

Farringay	...	...	...	...	1944	461	148	27	—	M(A)

ARTHUR GUINNESS, SON & CO. (DUBLIN) LTD.

DUBLIN

FUNNEL: *Red with black top. (Blue hulls).*

HOUSEFLAG: *Red swallowtail with large black letter "G".*

The Lady Grania	...	...	...	1952	1,152	213	35	11	M(A)
The Lady Gwendolen	...	...	1953	1,164	213	35	11	M(A)
The Lady Patricia	...	...	...	1963	1,187	213	38	11	M(A)

HARGREAVES COAL & SHIPPING CO. LTD.

HULL

FUNNEL: *Black with black "H" in white diamond on broad red band.*

HOUSEFLAG: *Red with black letter "H" in white diamond.*

Harfry	...	...	...	...	1952	1,231	229	35	—	M(A)
Harglen	...	...	...	...	1952	1,087	217	35	11½	M(A)

JOHN HARKER, LTD.

KNOTTINGLEY

FUNNEL: *Black with houseflag.*

HOUSEFLAG: *White with red letter "H" in red ring joined by a red stripe to top of hoist and bottom of fly.*

Coastal Tankers (Trading in Bristol Channel, Humber, and Tyne areas):
All single-screw motorships with engines aft:

Glaisdale H	303	Ribblesdale H	257	Waterdale H	278
Greendale H	311	Rosedale H	257	Weasdale H	270
Keeldale H	265	Southdale H	298	Westerndale H	223
Kendale	256	Teesdale H	298	Wheeldale H	273
Kerrydale H	255	Tynedale H	298	Wheldale H	250
Kingsdale H	276	Wandale H	262	Winsdale H	270
Kirkdale H	275	Wardale H	262	Wyesdale H	234

Also a large fleet of smaller river and esturial tankers.

HAY & CO. (LERWICK) LTD.
(SUBSIDIARY OF W. N. LINDSAY, LTD.)

LERWICK

FUNNEL: *Black with black letter "L" on red over white over blue bands.*

HOUSEFLAG: *Black "L" on bands as on funnel.*

Shetland Trader	...	...	...	1957	499	174	28	10	M(A)

J. HAY & SONS, LTD.
(SUBSIDIARY OF F. T. EVERARD & SONS, LTD., LONDON)

GLASGOW

FUNNEL: *Pink with black top.*

HOUSEFLAG:

Alfred Everard	...	...	...	1957	1,577	231	38	10	M(A)
The Duchess	...	...	...	1963	461	170	28	10	M(A)
The Marchioness	...	...	...	1935	324	136	25	8½	M(A)
The Marquis	...	...	...	1934	324	136	25	8½	M(A)
The Sultan	...	...	...	1950	524	174	28	9	M(A)

HEAD LINE
(G. HEYN & SONS, LTD.)
BELFAST

FUNNEL: *Black with red hand on white shield.*

HOUSEFLAG: *Blue with white letters "U"/S S Co. in the hoist and red hand on white shield in the fly.*

Ballygally Head	...	...	...	1954	959	242	38	12	M(A)
Benfore Head	...	...	...	1944	1,902	302	44	11	SR
Fair Head	...	...	...	1957	1,573	258	42	13½	M

HENRY & MACGREGOR, LTD.
LEITH

FUNNEL: *Black with two white bands.*

HOUSEFLAG: *Blue with blue letters "H & M" in red brodered white diamond.*

Cantick Head	...	...	...	1958	1,595	252	40	13½	M(A)
Dunnet Head	...	...	...	1953	749	193	31	10	M(A)
Kinnaird Head	...	...	...	1964	1,985	290	42	10½	M(A)
Marwick Head	...	...	...	1952	1,786	265	40	10	M(A)
Rattray Head	...	...	...	1965	1,600	274	—	—	M(A)
St. Abbs Head	...	...	...	1956	646	188	30	10½	M(A)

HINDLEA SHIPPING CO. LTD.
CARDIFF

FUNNEL:

HOUSEFLAG:

Linglea	...	...	...	...	1964	498	245	35	—	M(A)
Marshlea	...	...	...	...	1957	494	183	31	—	M(A)

HIGHSEAS LTD.
(ANTHONY & BAINBRIDGE, LTD.)
NEWCASTLE

FUNNEL: *Red with black top separated by broad white band.*

HOUSEFLAG:

Anglobel	...	...	...	...	1953	806	210	32	—	M(A)

M.V. Quiescence. London & Rochester Tdg Co. [*Fotoship*

M.V. Marwick Head. Henry & MacGregor Ltd. [*John G. Callis*

S.S. Ballymena. John Kelly Ltd. [*J. Clarkson*

HUDSON STEAMSHIP CO. LTD.

LONDON

FUNNEL: *Dark blue with white letter "H" on broad red band.*
HOUSEFLAG: *Blue with red letter "H" in white disc.*

Hudson Cape	...	...	...	1946	2,524	305	42	10	SR(A)
Hudson Firth	...	...	...	1949	3,117	337	45	10½	SR(A)
Hudson Light	...	...	...	1965	5,628	369	53	—	M(A)
Hudson River	...	...	...	1949	3,128	337	45	10½	SR(A)
Hudson Sound	...	...	...	1950	2,577	305	42	10	SR(A)
Hudson Strait	...	...	...	1946	3,105	337	45	10	SR(A)

Also larger ocean freighters.

HULL GATES SHIPPING CO. LTD.
(S. F. CRAGGS & CO.)

HULL

FUNNEL: *Yellow with narrow black top and houseflag.*
HOUSEFLAG: *Red bordered white pennant with red letters "H G".*

Foxtongate	...	...	...	1963	718	197	30	10	M(A)
Hesslegate	...	...	...	1947	547	182	27	—	M(A)
Irishgate	...	...	...	1965	790	200	32	—	M(A)
Kingsgate	...	...	...	1949	545	182	27	9½	M(A)
Northgate	...	...	...	1964	513	—	—	—	M(A)
Paullgate	...	...	...	1961	200	118	25	—	M(A)
Royalgate	...	...	...	1953	546	189	28	10	M(A)

GLYNWOOD NAVIGATION CO. LTD.

Heathergate	...	...	...	1957	597	180	29	9½	M(A)

IMPERIAL CHEMICAL INDUSTRIES LTD.

LONDON

FUNNEL: *Blue with black top and "ICI" device in white on red disc.*
HOUSEFLAG: *Blue with white "ICI" device.*

NOBEL DIVISION

Lady McGowan	...	...	...	1952	690	182	30	10½	M(A)
Lady Roslin	...	...	...	1958	708	175	32	10	M(A)

MOND DIVISION

Anderton	...	...	...	1946	216	103	23	7½	SR
Barnton	...	...	...	1944	216	103	23	7½	SR
Cerium	...	...	...	1948	532	181	29	—	M(A)
Comberbach	...	...	...	—	201	—	—	—	
Cuddington	...	...	...	1948	201	103	22	8	M(A)
Calcium	...	...	...	1959	644	183	32	10½	M(A)

Davenham	...	...	...	...	1946	216	103	23	7½	M(A)
James Jackson Grundy	...	...	1948	201	103	22	8	M
Marbury	...	...	...	...	1949	231	105	23	8	M(A)
Marston	...	...	...	...	1949	231	105	23	8	M(A)
Polythene	...	...	...	...	1949	330	140	25	9	M(A)
Weaverham	...	...	...	1948	201	103	22	8	M(A)
Wincham	...	...	...	...	1948	201	103	22	8	M(A)

Under 200 tons: **Decempedes** (1879/169 tons), **Frances Poole** (1923/175 tons)

INSTONE LINES, LTD.

LONDON

FUNNEL: *Black with red "I S" monogram on white disc on broad blue band.*
HOUSEFLAG: *As funnel band.*

Seashell	...	...	...	...	1943	423	177	26	—	M(A)

INTERNATIONAL SHIPBROKERS LTD.

LONDON

FUNNEL:
HOUSEFLAG:

Marinus V	...	...	...	...	1935	289	123*	24	10	M(A)

This company also operates a number of Dutch-flag coasters under charter.

T. G. IRVING, LTD.

SUNDERLAND

FUNNEL: *Black with red star on broad white band.*
HOUSEFLAG: *White with red border and large red five-pointed star.*

Ashdene	...	...	...	...	1931	162	99	22	—	M
Ferndene	...	...	...	...	1949	313	137	24	—	M(A)
Oakdene	...	...	...	...	1942	321	137	25	—	M(A)
Rosedene	...	...	...	...	1938	376	140	25	—	M(A)

ISLE OF MAN STEAM PACKET CO. LTD.

DOUGLAS, I.O.M.

FUNNEL: *Red with black top and black rings.*

HOUSEFLAG: *Red with Manx arms in yellow flanked by the yellow letters "I O M" and "S P C".*

SERVICES: *Douglas–Liverpool (Passenger and Cargo); Douglas to Heysham, Llandudno, Ardrossan, Belfast and Dublin; Liverpool to Llandudno (Passenger, Summer only).*

						Building			
Ben-my-Chree*	...	...	...	1951	1,019	223	37	12	M
Fenella	...	...	...	1946	2,485	345	47	21	ST(2)
King Orry	...	...	...	1946	2,485	345	47	21	ST(2)
Lady of Mann	...	...	...	1930	3,014	372	50	22½	ST(2)
Manx Maid*	...	...	...	1963	2,725	344	53	—	ST(2)
Manxman	...	...	...	1955	2,495	344	47	21	ST(2)
Mona's Isle	...	...	...	1951	2,491	345	47	21	ST(2)
Peveril	...	...	...	1964	1,048	220	41	—	M(A)
Snaefell	...	...	...	1948	2,489	345	47	21	ST(2)
Tynwald	...	...	...	1947	2,493	345	47	21	ST(2)

*Car Ferries.

ISLES OF SCILLY STEAMSHIP CO. LTD.

PENZANCE

FUNNEL: *Yellow.*

HOUSEFLAG:

SERVICES: *Penzance–Scilly Isles (Passenger and Cargo).*

Queen of the Isles	...	...	...	1965	600	—	—	—	M
Scillonian	...	...	...	1956	921	209	31	15	M(2)

JEPPESON-HEATON, LTD.

LONDON

FUNNEL:

HOUSEFLAG:

Con-Zelo	...	...	...	...	1957	400	165	26	10	M(A)

JOHN KELLY LTD.

BELFAST

FUNNEL: *Black with red over white over blue bands and small black letter "K" on white band. (Grey hulls).*

HOUSEFLAG: *Red swallowtail with blue border at top and bottom and large white letter "K".*

Ballyedward	...	...	...	1950	552	180	30	9	M(A)
Ballyhaft	...	...	...	1952	991	197	32	10	SR(A)
Ballyhill	...	...	...	1954	847	197	32	10	SR(A)
Ballylagan	...	...	...	1955	1,307	255	34	10	SR(A)
Ballylesson	...	...	...	1959	1,280	255	34	10½	M(A)
Ballyloran	...	...	...	1958	1,092	220	34	10½	M(A)
Ballylumford	...	...	...	1954	1,242	255	34	10	SR(A)
Ballymena	...	...	...	1954	1,340	240	38	10	SR(A)
Ballymoney	...	...	...	1953	1,342	240	38	10	SR(A)
Ballyrory	...	...	...	1963	1,575	256	39	10½	M(A)
Ballyrush	...	...	...	1962	1,575	256	39	10½	M(A)

KLONDYKE SHIPPING CO. LTD.

HULL

FUNNEL: *Grey with houseflag.*

HOUSEFLAG: *Red bordered yellow pennant with red letter "K".*

Framptondyke	...	...	...	1964	1,599	281	42	—	M(A)
Kirtondyke	...	...	...	1957	959	215	35	10	M(A)

KYLE SHIPPING CO. LTD.

(MONROE BROS.)

LIVERPOOL

FUNNEL: *Black with red over white band.*

HOUSEFLAG: *White with blue St. Andrew's cross with red diamond containing white letter "M" superimposed on centre.*

Kylebank	...	...	...	1961	1,143	228	36	11	M(A)
Kyle of Lochalsh	...	...	...	1952	1,224	229	35	11	M(A)

LEYLAND TANKERS, LTD.

LONDON

FUNNEL:

HOUSEFLAG:

SERVICES: *Thames tankers.*

Coastal Tankers:									
Mobilfuel	...	...	...	...	1955	425	158	30	—	M(A)
Mobilpet	...	...	...	...	1961	499	168	34	—	M(A)

LIGHT SHPG CO. LTD.
(ROSS & MARSHALL LTD.)

GREENOCK

FUNNEL: *Red with black top separated by white band.*

HOUSEFLAG:

Polarlight	...	...	...	...	1959	200	118	25	—	M(A)

Under 200 tons: **Limelight** (1916/143 tons), **Moonlight** (1952/164 tons), **Raylight** (1963/177 tons), **Stormlight** (1957/166 tons) and **Warlight** (1920/137 tons).

W. N. LINDSAY, LTD.
LEITH

FUNNEL: *Red with black top and blue band.*

HOUSEFLAG:

Karri ...	...	...	...	...	1938	354	147	24	10	M(A)
Roseburn	...	...	...	...	1947	604	197	28	9½	M(A)
Roselyne	...	...	...	...	1939	417	152	26	9¾	M(A)
Rosemarkie		...	...	...	1939	499	159	27	9	M(A)
Roseheath	...	...	...	...	1949	1,366	235	36	10	M(A)

LINK LINES, LTD.
(COAST LINES GROUP)
LIVERPOOL

FUNNEL: *Black with green-bordered red chevron.*

HOUSEFLAG:

SERVICES: *Irish Sea container services from Liverpool.*

Bison†	...	...	...	...	1961	2,144	258	42	—	M(A)
Buffalo†	...	...	...	...	1961	2,163	258	42	—	M(A)
Pointer*	...	...	...	...	1956	1,208	224	37	11½	M(A)
Spaniel*	...	...	...	...	1955	1,206	224	38	11½	M(A)
Terrier†	...	...	...	...	1957	1,098	220	35	—	M(A)

† Owned by Coast Lines Ltd.   * Owned by Burns & Laird Lines.

LONDON & ROCHESTER TRADING CO. LTD.

ROCHESTER

FUNNEL: *Black with white crescent on broad red band bordered by two narrow white bands. (Reddish-brown hulls).*

HOUSEFLAG: *Red with white crescent.*

SERVICES: *Whitstable–Ebsjerg (Cargo).*

Crescence	...	...	...	...	1965	950	221	35	—	M(A)
Dominence	...	...	...	...	1940	261	119	25	8	M(A)
Elation	...	...	...	...	1963	212	99	22	—	M(A)
Eminence	...	...	...	...	1945	555	174	28	10	M(A)
Faience	...	...	...	...	1943	552	188	27	10¼	M(A)
Function	...	...	...	...	1963	210	99	22	—	M(A)
Gardience	...	...	...	...	1948	552	188	27	10½	M(A)
Halcience	...	...	...	...	1949	994	220	33	10	M(A)
Insistence	...	...	...	...	1939	288	131	24	9½	M(A)
Jubilence	...	...	...	...	1950	515	174	28	9	M(A)
Kindrence	...	...	...	...	1950	522	175	28	10	M(A)
Luminence	...	...	...	...	1954	558	190	28	10½	M(A)
Militence	...	...	...	...	1956	560	191	28	10½	M(A)
Ordinence	...	...	...	...	1941	321	137	25	—	M(A)
Pertinence	...	...	...	...	1959	868	206	32	10½	M(A)
Quiescence	...	...	...	...	1959	867	206	32	10½	M(A)
Resurgence	...	...	...	...	1958	499	219	32	10½	M(A)

Under 200 tons: **Action Bastion, Diction, Gillation, Gold, Marie May, Naughton, Nicola Dawn, Pepita, Servic, Silver,** and others.

COMBEN LONGSTAFF & CO. LTD.

LONDON

FUNNEL: *Black with red "C L" on white diamond on broad red band.*

HOUSEFLAG: *Red with white diamond containing red letters "C L",*

Caernarvonbrook	...	...	...	1964	1,594	265	39	12	M(A)
Cardiffbrook	...	...	...	1952	1,812	273	38	11½	M(A)
Cardiganbrook	...	...	...	1952	1,780	273	38	11	M(A)
Chesterbrook	...	...	...	1963	1,594	265	39	12	M(A)
Clarebrook	...	...	...	1964	1,594	265	39	12	M(A)
Cornishbrook	...	...	...	1964	1,595	265	39	12	M(A)
Corkbrook	...	...	...	1964	1,594	265	39	12	M(A)
Dorsetbrook	...	...	...	1957	1,328	235	36	11	M(A)
Durhambrook	...	...	...	1955	1,275	236	35	11½	M(A)
Warwickbrook	...	...	...	1958	1,035	217	34	11¼	M(A)
Westminsterbrook	...	...	...	1961	1,040	217	34	11¼	M(A)
Winchesterbrook	...	...	...	1960	1,035	219	34	11¼	M(A)
Worcesterbrook	...	...	...	1958	1,023	220	34	11¼	M(A)

M.V. Ann M. Metcalf Motor Coasters. [*W. J. Harris*

S.S. John Orwell Philips. North Thames Gas Board. [*A. Duncan*

M.V. Osborne Queen. Queenship Nav. Co. Ltd. [*John G. Callis*
(Now owned by the Britain S.S. Co.)

DAVID MACBRAYNE, LTD.

GLASGOW

FUNNEL: *Red with black top.*

HOUSEFLAG: *Blue pennant with red St. Andrew's cross in hoist and similar white cross at centre.*

SERVICES: *Glasgow to Oban, Fort William, Inverness and the Western Islands. Inter-Island services and ferries.*

Clansman†	...	...	...	...	1964	2,104	235	46	—	M
Claymore	...	...	...	...	1955	1,024	192	35	12½	M
Columba†	...	...	...	...	1964	2,104	235	46	—	M
Hebrides†	...	...	...	...	1964	2,104	235	46	—	M
King George V	...	...	...	1926	815	270	32	16	ST(2)
Loch Ard	...	...	...	...	1955	611	184	34	12	M(A)
Lochbroom	...	...	...	...	1946	325	151	27	10	M(A)
Loch Carron	...	...	...	...	1951	683	203	34	11	M(A)
Loch Dunvegan	...	...	...	1946	528	190	31	10	M(A)
Lochfyne	...	...	...	...	1931	754	219	30	14½	ME(2)
Lochiel	...	...	...	...	1939	603	191	32	13	M(2)
Lochnevis	...	...	...	...	1934	568	179	31	14	ME(2)
Loch Seaforth	...	...	...	...	1947	1,090	241	36	14	M(2)

Under 200 tons: **Loch Arkaig** (179 tons), **Loch Eynort** (117 tons), and the smaller **Lochallort, Lochbuie, Lochnell,** and **Loch Toscaig.**

David MacBrayne, Ltd., is controlled jointly by the British Transport Commission and Coast Lines Ltd. † Owned by Secretary of State for Scotland and managed by MacBraynes.

P. MACCALLUM & SONS, LTD.

GREENOCK

FUNNEL: *Red with black top and black rings. (Grey hulls).*

HOUSEFLAG: *Divided vertically red in the hoist and blue in the fly with a large six pointed white star in the centre.*

Ardgarvel	...	...	...	...	1965	1,120	223	35	12	M(A)
Ardglen	...	...	...	...	1953	1,044	221	34	10½	M(A)

METCALF MOTOR COASTERS, LTD.

LONDON

FUNNEL: *Green with large white letter "M".*

HOUSEFLAG: *White bordered green swallowtail with large white letter "M".*

Ann M.	...	...	...	...	1962	1,203	230	37	11	M(A)
Christopher M.	...	...	...	1956	1,035	217	34	11	M(A)
Ellen M.	...	...	...	...	1936	534	191	27	8½	M(A)
Marian M.	...	...	...	...	1955	694	195	32	11	M(A)
Melissa M.	...	...	...	...	1956	1,089	230	34	12	M(A)
Michael M.	...	...	...	...	1955	691	198	31	10	M(A)
Moira M.	...	...	...	...	1937	678	187	30	—	M(A)

Monica M.	...	...	...	...	1936	534	190	27	—	M(A)
Polly M.	...	...	...	...	1937	360	147	26	8½	M(A)
Thomas M.	...	...	...	...	1938	507	173	27	9	M(A)

Coastal Tankers:

Adrian M.	...	...	...	...	1957	967	217	32	11	M(A)
Anthony M.	...	...	...	...	1944	465	159	26	9½	M(A)
Caroline M.	...	...	...	...	1935	1,598	255	42	10½	M(A)
Frank M.	...	...	...	...	1965	1,300	230	37	—	M(A)
John M.	...	...	...	...	1963	1,300	230	37	—	M(A)
Nicholas M.	...	...	...		—	1,300	—	—	—	M(A)

MAC SHIPPING CO. LTD.

Daniel M.	...	...	...	...	1936	450	156	26	8½	M(A)

WIMAISIA SHIPPING CO. LTD.

David M.	...	...	...	...	1933	350	137	55	9	M(A)

MONROE BROS. LTD.

LIVERPOOL

See Kyle Shipping Co. Ltd.

W. G. MORAY & CO. LTD.

GARSTON

FUNNEL:

HOUSEFLAG:

Manta	...	...	...	...	1951	366	149	24	10	M(A)

Wm. H. MULLER & CO. (LONDON) LTD.

LONDON

FUNNEL: *Black with large white "M" on broad red band between two narrow white bands.*

HOUSEFLAG: *White field, with the white letters "Wm. H. M. & Co." between two narrow white bands on a broad red band.*

Meuse	...	...	...	...	1953	430	161	25	—	M(A)
Scheldt	...	...	...	...	1959	397	153	25	—	M(A)
Somme	...	...	...	...	1950	451	161	25	—	M(A)

The parent company Wm. H. Muller & Co., operates under the Dutch flag.

NEWCASTLE COAL & SHIPPING CO. LTD.

LONDON

FUNNEL: *Black with red and white houseflag.*

HOUSEFLAG:

Camroux III	...	...	...	1935	409	170	26	9½	M(A)

NORTH EASTERN FISHERIES LTD.

ABERDEEN

FUNNEL:

HOUSEFLAG:

Mount Battock	...	...	...	1939	396	147	26	—	SR(A)

NORTH OF SCOTLAND, ORKNEY & SHETLAND SHIPPING CO. LTD.
(COAST LINES GROUP)

ABERDEEN

FUNNEL: *Yellow.*

HOUSEFLAG: *Divided horizontally blue over white over blue.*

SERVICES: *Leith and Aberdeen to Kirkwall and Lerwick; Leith, Aberdeen and Stromness to St. Margaret's Hope; Aberdeen to Lerwick; Lerwick to North Isles of Shetland; and Thurso (Scrabster) to Stromness (Passenger and Cargo).*

Earl of Zetland	...	...	...	1939	548	166	29	12	M
St. Clair	...	...	...	1960	3,303	296	50	13	M
St. Clement	...	...	...	1946	460	188	31	12	M(A)
St. Magnus	...	...	...	1937	1,641	266	38	14	SR
St. Ninian	...	...	...	1950	2,242	286	46	15	M(2)
St. Ola	...	...	...	1951	750	178	33	12	M
St. Rognvald	...	...	...	1955	1,024	244	39	13	M(A)

NORTH THAMES GAS BOARD

LONDON

FUNNEL: *Black with band of red pyramids over two narrow black bands all on a broad white band.*

HOUSEFLAG: *White with red rising sun device in centre and the blue letters "N T G B" in each corner.*

Accum*	...	...	...	1950	1,771	271	40	11	M(A)
Adams Beck*	...	...	...	1949	1,773	271	40	10½	M(A)

David Pollock	...	...	...	1954	3,332	339	46	10½	SR(A)
Falconer Birks*	...	...	...	1953	1,762	271	40	11	M(A)
Firebeam*	...	...	...	1945	1,554	257	40	10	SR(A)
Frederick John Evans	...	...	1954	3,375	344	46	10½	SR(A)
John Orwell Philips	...	...	1955	3,378	344	46	10½	SR(A)
Murdoch*	...	...	...	1949	1,759	271	39	10½	M(A)
Samuel Clegg*	...	...	...	1950	1,773	271	40	10	M(A)
Sir David II	...	...	...	1954	3,332	339	46	10½	SR(A)
Thomas Goulden	...	...	...	1955	3,332	339	46	10½	SR(A)
Thomas Hardie*	...	...	...	1950	1,771	271	40	10	M(A)
Thomas Livesey*	...	...	...	1953	1,779	271	40	11	M(A)

* Up-River Collier or "Flatiron."

NORTHERN CO-OPERATIVE SOCIETY LTD.

ABERDEEN

FUNNEL: *Yellow with black top separated by red band.*

HOUSEFLAG:

Thrift	...	...	...	...	1931	648	183	28	10½	SR(A)

NORTHERN SHIPPING & TRADING CO. (HELMSDALE) LTD.

ABERDEEN

FUNNEL:

HOUSEFLAG:

Helmsdale	...	...	...	...	1956	402	153	26	9½	M(A)

ORKNEY ISLANDS SHIPPING CO. LTD.

KIRKWALL

FUNNEL: *Red with white "I O" monogram between two narrow white bands.*

HOUSEFLAG:

SERVICES: *Inter-island (Passenger and Cargo).*

Earl Sigurd	...	...	...	...	1931	221	119	24	—	SR
Orcadia*	...	...	...	...	1963	896	164	37	—	M

* Owned by the Secretary of State for Scotland.

M.V. Ben Varrey. Ramsey S.S. Co. [*J. Clarkson*

M.V. Magrix. J. R. Rix & Sons. [*John G. Callis*

M.V. Anchorman. C. Rowbotham. [*John G. Callis*

OSBORN & WALLIS LTD.

BRISTOL

FUNNEL: *Red with black top.*

HOUSEFLAG: *White with blue "O W" monogram.*

Brandon	...	...	...	...	1957	586	170	29	9	M(A)
Colston	...	...	...	...	1955	586	170	29	9	M(A)
Hotwells	...	...	...	...	1950	499	163	27	9	M(A)
St. Vincent	...	...	...	...	1940	484	162	27	9	M(A)
Salcombe	...	...	...	...	1938	590	170	27	9	M(A)

J. J. PRIOR (TRANSPORT) LTD.

LONDON

FUNNEL: *Red with black top.*

HOUSEFLAG:

Colne Trader	...	...	...	1941	329	136	25	9	M(A)

Under 200 tons: **A.H.P.** (1917/175 tons), **Bert Prior** (1965/175 tons), **James P.** (1963/191 tons), **Leah P.** (1915/172 tons), **Leonard P.** (1915/174 tons), **Peter P.** (1915/186 tons) and **Sidney P.** (1916/162 tons)

RAMSEY STEAMSHIP CO. LTD.

RAMSEY, I.O.M.

FUNNEL: *Black with white Maltese cross on red band. (Grey hulls).*

HOUSEFLAG:

Ben Rein	...	...	...	...	1947	393	149	26	10	M(A)
Ben Varrey	...	...	...	...	1963	451	174	26	—	M(A)
Ben Veg	...	...	...	...	1965	440	144	26	—	M(A)
Ben Vooar	...	...	...	...	1950	441	160	27	8½	M(A)

REGENT OIL CO. LTD.

LONDON

FUNNEL: *Black with "Regent" emblem on red over white over blue bands. (Grey hulls).*

HOUSEFLAG:

Coastal Tanker:									
Regent Jane ...	...	...	...	1952	376	150	27	—	M(A)

Under 200 tons: **Regent Linnet, Regent Robin, Regent Swallow, Regent Swift** and **Regent Wren.** (All 100/160 tons. Bristol Channel Coastal Tankers)

J. R. RIX & SONS LTD.

HULL

FUNNEL: *Red with blue top with white "J R" monogram on red diamond. (Green hulls).*

HOUSEFLAG: *Blue with white "J R" monogram on red diamond.*

Bobrix	...	...	...	...	1957	584	180	29	10	M(A)
Fylrix	...	...	...	...	1962	598	189	28	10	M(A)
Jonrix	...	...	...	...	1957	584	180	29	10	M(A)
Kenrix	...	...	...	...	1960	592	189	28	10	M(A)
Lesrix	...	...	...	...	1957	676	185	33	10	M(A)

THOMAS ROSE & CO. LTD.

SUNDERLAND

FUNNEL: *Black with blue "x" on broad white band.*

HOUSEFLAG:

Edenside	...	...	...	...	1941	316	137	25	8	M(A)

CHRISTOPHER ROWBOTHAM & SONS LTD.

LONDON

FUNNEL: *Yellow with red "R" and narrow black top.*

HOUSEFLAG: *Blue with red letter "R" on white diamond.*

Coastal Tankers:	THE BRIDGEMAN SHIPPING CO. LTD.								
Bridgeman	...	...	...	...	1939	369	154	26	8	M(A)
Steersman	...	...	...	...	1936	334	152	24	7	M(A)
Tillerman	...	...	...	...	1963	807	203	31	10	M(A)
Wheelsman	...	...	...	...						

THE QUARTERMAN SHIPPING CO. LTD.

Chartsman	...	...	...	1944	340	152	24	8	M(A)
Oarsman	...	...	...	1959	778	204	31	10½	M(A)
Quarterman...	...	...	...	1953	470	179	28	10	M(A)

THE HELMSMAN SHIPPING CO. LTD.

Anchorman	...	...	...	1962	795	203	31	10	M(A)
Guidesman	...	...	...	1938	233	119	23	7	M(A)
Helmsman	...	...	...	1937	493	176	26	8	M(A)
Pointsman	...	...	...	1934	1,174	233	35	7	SR(A)
Rudderman	...	...	...	1934	290	138	23	7	M(A)

Chr. SALVESEN & CO. LTD.
LEITH

FUNNEL : *Red with blue top separated by broad white band.*

HOUSEFLAG : *White, with white-edged blue cross on red diamond.*

Fidra	...	...	...	...	1956	1,333	230	35	10½	M(A)
Glitra	...	...	...	...	1952	991	221	35	10½	M(A)
Laksa	...	...	...	...	1960	1,323	230	35	11½	M(A)
Logna	...	...	...	...	1958	1,341	228	35	10½	M(A)
Otra	...	...	...	...	1957	1,325	229	35	10½	M(A)
Soutra	...	...	...	...	1958	1,334	229	35	11½	M(A)
Tolsta	...	...	...	...	1960	1,323	230	35	11½	M)A)

Also larger Ocean Freighters, Whaling Ships, and Factory Trawlers.

W. A. SAVAGE LTD.
(COAST LINES GROUP)
LIVERPOOL

FUNNEL : *Yellow with black top.*

HOUSEFLAG : *Divided vertically blue, white and blue, with red letter "Z" on white.*

Earlsfield	...	...	...	...	1952	635	200	30	10½	M(A)
Fallowfield	...	...	...	...	1953	566	198	30	10½	M(A)
Fernfield	...	...	...	...	1954	561	200	30	10	M(A)
Foxfield	...	...	...	...	1952	546	189	30	10	M(A)
Grangefield	...	...	...	...	1954	504	175	28	10¼	M(A)
Greenfield	...	...	...	...	1953	504	175	28	10¼	M(A)
Holmfield	...	...	...	...	1957	488	169	28	9	M(A)
Oatfield	...	...	...	...	1952	538	175	27	10	M(A)

SHAMROCK SHIPPING CO. LTD.
LARNE

FUNNEL : *Black with yellow letter "S".*

HOUSEFLAG :

Clonlee	...	...	...	1959	643	—	—	—	—
Loch Etive	...	...	...	1948	982	218	32	—	M(A)

M.V. Tolsta. Chr. Salvesen & Co. [*Fotoship*

M.V. Ben Hittinger, funnel colours have since been changed. Shell Mex & B.P. Ltd
[*John G. Callis*

M.V. Greenland. Shipping & Coal Co. [*John G. Callis*

J. SHAW
GLOUCESTER

FUNNEL: *Yellow with red letter "S".*

HOUSEFLAG:

Arlingham	...	...	...	1934	268	122*	22	9	M(A)

SHELL-MEX & B.P., LTD.
LONDON

FUNNEL: *Black with yellow band between two white bands.*

HOUSEFLAG:

Coastal Tankers:

B.P. Haulier	...	...	...	1956	315	148	28	7½	M(A)
B.P. Manager	...	...	...	1944	1,149	241	34	9½	SR(A)
B.P. Manufacturer	...	...	...	1943	303	139	22	8	M(A)
B.P. Miller	...	...	...	1956	301	139	22	8	M(A)
B.P. Supervisor	...	...	...	1946	860	202	34	10	M(A)
Ben Bates	...	...	...	1956	565	181	28	10½	M(A)
Ben Harold Smith	...	...	...	1952	325	136	26	8½	M(A)
Ben Hittinger	...	...	...	1951	522	181	28	10½	M(A)
Falmouth	...	...	...	1965	1,000	202	34	—	M(A)
Fealtie	...	...	...	1928	351	153	24	9	M(A)
Hamble	...	...	...	1964	1,182	215	37	10½	M(A)
Killingholme	...	...	...	1964	1,182	216	37	10½	M(A)
Pando	...	...	...	1921	313	131	26	7	SR(A)
Partington	...	...	...	1966	1,000	202	34	—	M(A)
Perso	...	...	...	1921	313	131	26	7	SR(A)
Phero	...	...	...	1921	325	131	26	7	SR(A)
Philo	...	...	...	1921	338	147	24	7	SR(A)
Poilo	...	...	...	1921	307	146	24	7	SR(A)
St. Leonards	...	...	...			Building			
Shell Director	...	...	...	1946	891	201	32	9½	M(A)
Shell Dispenser	...	...	...	1963	239	133	27	—	M(A)
Shell Driller	...	...	...	1946	969	202	34	10	M(A)
Shell Farmer	...	...	...	1955	313	138	29	8	M(A)
Shell Glassmaker	...	...	...	1957	303	139	22	8	M(A)
Shell Roadbuilder	...	...	...	1956	301	139	22	8	M(A)
Shell Steelmaker	...	...	...	1956	301	139	22	8	M(A)
Shell Supplier	...	...	...	1946	1,157	241	24	9½	SR(A)
Shell Traveller	...	...	...	1958	303	139	22	8	M(A)
Shell Welder	...	...	...	1955	569	171	30	8½	M(A)
Torksey	...	...	...	1964	230	117	27	—	M(A)

Under 200 tons: **British Maiden** (1942/102 tons), **British Toiler** (1925/131 tons), **Jorie** (1925/130 tons), **Shell Mex 3** (1916/128 tons), **Ben Olliver** (1935/147 tons)

SHIPPING & COAL CO. LTD.
LONDON

FUNNEL: *Black with blue diamond on broad white band between two narrow red bands.*

HOUSEFLAG: *Blue with three horizontal red stripes the middle one interrupted by a white diamond containing the blue letters "S C C".*

Greenland	...	...	...	...	1962	2,200	285	43	11	M(A)
Queensland	...	...	...	...	1958	2,750	336	45	11	M(A)
Waterland	...	...	...	...	1950	2,837	314	45	11	M(A)

The associated Dutch company, Scheepvaarten-Steenkolen Maats N.V., operated coasters under the Netherlands flag.

Wm. SLOAN & CO. LTD.
(COAST LINES GROUP)
GLASGOW

FUNNEL: *Black with broad white band.*
HOUSEFLAG: *Blue with large white diamond containing the red letters "W S & Co."*
SERVICES: *Glasgow to Belfast, Dublin, South Wales ports and Bristol (Cargo).*

Talisker	...	...	...	...	1955	1,016	247	38	11	M(A)
Tay ...	...	...	...	...	1951	791	234	35	11½	M(A)
Kelvin	...	...	...	...	1955	979	252	38	11	M(A)

SOUTH EASTERN GAS BOARD
LONDON

FUNNEL: *Black with red band having letters "S E G B" in blue on white panel between two white and red bands.*
HOUSEFLAG: *As funnel band.*

Camberwell ...	...	...	...	1958	1,877	275	39	11	M(A)
Catford	...	...	...	...	1948	2,724	319	44	10½	M(A)
Chessington ...	...	...	...	1946	1,720	271	40	10	SR(A)
Croydon	...	...	...	...	1951	1,871	275	40	10½	M(A)
Dulwich*	...	...	...	...	1957	1,873	275	39	11	M(A)
Effra	...	...	...	...	1946	2,701	319	44	10	SR(A)
Ewell*	...	...	...	...	1958	1,877	275	39	11	M(A)
Kingston*	...	...	...	...	1956	1,873	275	39	11	M(A)
Lambeth*	...	...	...	...	1958	1,877	275	39	11	M(A)
Mitcham*	...	...	...	...	1946	1,787	271	40	10½	M(A)
Southwark ...	...	...	...	1958	3,070	320	44	11	M(A)
Sydenham ...	...	...	...	1951	1,871	275	40	10½	M(A)
Wandsworth*	...	...	...	1950	1,875	275	40	10½	M(A)

* Up-River Collier.

SOUTHAMPTON, ISLE OF WIGHT & SOUTH OF ENGLAND ROYAL MAIL S. P. CO. LTD.
SOUTHAMPTON

FUNNEL: *Red with black top.*
HOUSEFLAG: *Quartered diagonally, white, blue, green, and red.*
SERVICES: *Southampton to Cowes (Passenger and Car Ferry); Excursions from Southampton.*

Balmoral	...	...	...	...	1949	688	204	30	15	M(2)
Carisbrook Castle ...	...	...	...	1959	620	191	42	14	M(2)
Osborne Castle	...	...	...	1962	736	188	42	14	M(2)
Vecta	...	...	...	...	1938	630	200	30	14	M(2)

The company also operates a fleet of tugs and tenders in Southampton Docks.

M.V. Kelvin. Wm. Sloan & Co. [*Fotoship*

M.V. Vecta. Southampton, Isle of Wight & South of England S.P. Co.
[*W. Paul Clegg*

M.V. Midhurst. Stephenson Clarke Ltd. [*A. Duncan*

SPRINGWELL SHIPPING CO. LTD.

ABERDEEN

FUNNEL: *Black with black triangle on white disc on broad blue band between two white bands.*

HOUSEFLAG:

Springfinch ...	...	...	...	1964	331	145	26	—	M(A)

STEPHENSON CLARKE LTD.

LONDON

FUNNEL: *Black with silver band.*

HOUSEFLAG: *Blue with red St. Andrew's cross and white letters "S C" in middle quarters.*

Abbas*	...	...	...	...	1955	953	207	31	—	M(A)
Amberley	...	...	...	...	1955	1,934	262	39	10½	M(A)
Ardingley	...	...	...	...	1951	1,473	253	37	10½	M(A)
Arundel	...	...	...	...	1956	3,422	344	46	10½	SR(A)
Beeding	...	...	...	...	1950	1,142	225	35	11	M(A)
Borde ...	...	...	...	...	1943	3,401	344	46	10½	SR(A)
Bowcombe	...	...	...	...	1943	2,760	322	45	10	SR(A)
Bramber	...	...	...	...	1954	2,480	265	40	9½	SR(A)
Broadhurst	...	...	...	...	1948	1,098	225	35	11	M(A)
Cowdray	...	...	...	...	1959	1,748	245	40	12	M(A)
Emsworth	...	...	...	...	1950	1,784	267	38	11	M(A)
Findon	...	...	...	...	1957	3,432	344	46	10½	M(A)
Gosport	...	...	...	...	1952	1,824	262	39	10½	M(A)
Hayling	...	...	...	...	1953	1,837	262	39	10½	M(A)
Henfield	...	...	...	...	1949	1,098	225	35	10½	M(A)
Heyshott	...	...	...	...	1949	2,918	329	35	10	SR(A)
Horsted	...	...	...	...	1945	2,960	284	41	10	SR(A)
Keynes	...	...	...	...	1946	1,563	270	36	10½	SR(A)
Lancing	...	...	...	...	1958	1,638	242	38	11	M(A)
Minster	...	...	...	...	1950	3,194	335	46	11	M(A)
Portslade	...	...	...	...	1955	1,797	242	40	11	M(A)
Portsmouth	...	...	...	...	1950	1,805	268	38	10½	M(A)
Pulborough	...	...	...	...	1965	4,800	370	53	—	M(A)
Seaford	...	...	...	...	1947	1,062	225	35	10½	M(A)
Shoreham	...	...	...	...	1957	1,834	242	41	12	M(A)
Steyning	...	...	...	...	1955	1,637	242	38	10¾	M(A)
Storrington	...	...	...	...	1959	3,809	345	49	—	M(A)
Totland	...	...	...	...	1952	1,570	242	38	11½	M(A)
Coastal Tankers:									
Chailey	...	...	...	...	1957	2,175	287	42	11	M(A)
Fernhurst	...	...	...	...	1960	1,760	230	40	10½	M(A)
Firle ...	...	...	...	...	1958	948	211	34	9	M(A)
Friston	...	...	...	...	1959	948	211	35	9	M(A)
Maplehurst	...	...	...	...	1961	1,760	230	40	10½	M(A)
Midhurst	...	...	...	...	1960	1,760	230	40	10½	M(A)
Petworth	...	...	...	...	1958	1,266	233	35	10½	M(A)
Stansted	...	...	...	...	1957	1,034	223	34	11	M(A)

Also larger ocean freighters. * Liquefied Gas Carrier.

JOHN STEWART & CO. LTD.
GLASGOW

FUNNEL: *Black with pale band between two white rings.*
HOUSEFLAG: *Red with white "S" in white-edged blue diamond.*

Yewarch	...	...	...	...	1957	967	214	35	10½	M(A)
Yewdale	...	...	...	...	1949	987	221	34	10½	M(A)
Yewforest	...	...	...	...	1958	1,090	222	35	10½	M(A)
Yewhill	...	...	...	...	1957	1,089	221	35	10½	M(A)
Yewmount	...	...	...	...	1955	1,050	221	34	10½	M(A)
Yewpark	...	...	...	...	1944	1,596	258	39	10½	M(A)
Yewtree	...	...	...	...	1954	1,113	218	35	10½	M(A)

THOS. STONE (SHIPPING) LTD.
SWANSEA

FUNNEL:
HOUSEFLAG:

Friendship	...	...	...	...	1957	560	200	31	—	M(A)

JOHN SUMMERS & SONS, LTD.
SHOTTON

FUNNEL: *Black with blue letter "S" on red bordered white diamond interrupting red-edged white band.*

HOUSEFLAG:

Hawarden Bridge	...	...	...	1940	297	138	25	—	M(A)
Staley Bridge	...	...	...	1940	297	138	25	—	M(A)

G. T. SYMONS (AGENCIES) LTD.
LONDON

FUNNEL:
HOUSEFLAG:
SERVICES: *London–Paris (Cargo).*

Anjou	...	...	...	...	1958	481	176	25	—	M(A)
Normandy	...	...	...	...	1949	394	170	24	—	M(A)
Seine	...	...	...	...	1949	385	170	24	—	M(A)

M. P. TAYLOR
LEITH

FUNNEL: *Black.*
HOUSEFLAG:

Reedwarbler	...	...	...	1951	375	148	25	—	M(A)

S.S. Rogate. Stephenson Clarke Ltd. [*John G. Callis*

M.V. Yewdale. J. Stewart & Co. Shpg. [*Fotoship*

G. W. THACKER, LTD.
NEWCASTLE

FUNNEL:

HOUSEFLAG:

Kingham	...	...	...	...	1949	2,002	297	40	—	SR

TOWNSEND BROS. FERRIES, LTD.
DOVER

FUNNEL: *Red with black top.*

HOUSEFLAG:

SERVICES: *Dover–Calais (Car Ferry).*

Free Enterprise*	...	...	1962	2,607	316	54	—	M(2)
Free Enterprise II*	...	...	1965	3,000	355	60	—	M(2)
Free Enterprise III*	...	...			Building			

* Car Ferries.

E. W. TURNER & SON
LIVERPOOL

FUNNEL: *Red with narrow black top and large white letter "T".*

HOUSEFLAG:

Mertola	...	...	...	...	1950	497	172	28	10	M(A)

TYNE-TEES STEAM SHIPPING CO. LTD.
(COAST LINES GROUP)
NEWCASTLE

FUNNEL: *Black with white over red band.*

HOUSEFLAG: *Red with yellow lion and castle device in centre.*

SERVICES: *Newcastle–Hamburg (Passenger and Cargo); Newcastle and Middlesbrough to Dutch, Belgian and Northern French ports, Newcastle–Channel Islands, Newcastle–London (Cargo).*

Cyprian Coast	...	...	...	1936	508	172	27	9	M(A)
Frisian Coast	...	...	...	1937	586	196	32	11	M(A)
Iberian Coast	...	...	...	1950	1,188	220	36	11	M(A)
Netherlands Coast	...	...	...	1953	867	226	37	12	M(A)
Novian Coast	...	...	...	1936	507	172	27	9	M(A)
Olivian Coast	...	...	...	1946	749	211	33	12	M(A)
Yorkshire Coast	...	...	...	1959	750	196	33	11	M(A)

UNION LIGHTERAGE CO. LTD.

LONDON

FUNNEL: *Black.*

HOUSEFLAG:

SERVICES: *Thames and Medway tanker trades.*

Thames Tankers:

Astro ...	...	...	...	...	1964	551	176	34	—	M(A)
B.P. Spirit	...	...	...	1939	440	162	32	—	M(A)
Petro ...	...	...	...	...	1939	444	162	32	—	M(A)
Shell Spirit I ...	...	...	...	1938	440	162	32	—	M(A)
Shell Spirit II	...	...	...	1939	440	162	32	—	M(A)
Toro ...	...	...	...	...	1961	512	171	34	—	M(A)
Ulco ...	...	...	...	...	1958	507	172	34	—	M(A)

Under 200 tons: **Banco** (1927/107 tons), **Lectro** (1933/120 tons)

UNITED BALTIC CORPORATION

LONDON

FUNNEL: *Pale yellow with narrow black top and houseflag device on black edged white disc.*

HOUSEFLAG: *White with red anchor and red letters "U B C"*

SERVICES: *London, Hull and other U.K. ports to Gdynia, Helsinki, Kotka, Turku, Mantyluoto, Leningrad and Riga.*

Baltic Arrow	...	...	...	1956	1,385	291	40	14½	M(A)
Baltic Clipper	...	...	...	1954	1,198	285	38	14	M(A)
Baltic Comet	...	...	...	1954	1,198	285	38	14	M(A)
Baltic Exporter	...	...	...	1953	1,665	317	42	15	M
Baltic Express	...	...	...	1958	2,041	333	45	15¾	M
Baltic Importer	...	...	...	1953	1,683	325	42	15	M
Baltic Jet ...	...	...	...	1959	1,670	299	41	13½	M
Baltic Merchant	...	...	...	1954	1,689	325	42	15	M
Baltic Sprite	...	...	...	1960	960	263	41	13	M(A)
Baltic Star ...	...	...	...	1961	1,571	305	42	14	M(A)
Baltic Sun ...	...	...	...	1962	3,531	390	56	—	M(A)
Baltic Swift ...	...	...	...	1957	1,374	291	41	13	M(A)
Baltic Trader	...	...	...	1954	1,689	325	42	15	M
Baltic Venture	...	...	...	1965	1,581	280	46	15	M(A)
Baltrover ...	...	...	...	1949	2,179	350	51	14	SR

VACUUM OIL CO. LTD.

LONDON

FUNNEL: *Black with red winged horse device on white shield.*

HOUSEFLAG:

Coastal Tanker:								
Vacuum Pioneer	...	...	...	1953	1,650	260	40	11¼	M(A)

THOMAS WATSON (SHIPPING) LTD.

ROCHESTER

FUNNEL: *Yellow with pale blue band between two red bands. (Blue hulls).*

HOUSEFLAG:

Lady Sandra	...	...	...	1958	356	149	24	10	M(A)
Lady Serena	...	...	...	1964	200	137	25	—	M(A)
Lady Sybilla ...	...	...	...	1952	359	149	24	10	M(A)

Under 200 tons: **Lady Sonia** (1929/199 tons), **Lady Sarita** (1965/199 tons)

WESTERN SHIPPING LTD.

JERSEY

See Channel Shipping Ltd., Jersey

J. WHARTON (SHIPPING) LTD.

FUNNEL: *Black with black "W" on red diamond on broad yellow band.*

HOUSEFLAG:

Burtonia	...	...	...	...	1960	498	178	29	10	M(A)
Gladonia	...	...	...	...	1963	660	186	29	—	M(A)
Trentonia	...	...	...	...	1965	570	177	30	10	M(A)
Tryonia	...	...	...	...	1949	481	174	28	10	M(A)

JOHN H. WHITAKER (TANKERS) LTD.

HULL

FUNNEL: *Black with separate red and green bands.*

HOUSEFLAG: *Green and red pennant with white "W" on red disc on green*

Coastal Tanker:									
Whitonia	...	...	...	...	1950	315	143*	20	—	M(A)

Under 200 tons: A large fleet of smaller tankers and dry cargo vessels operates on inland waterways from Hull.

C. M. WILLIE & CO. (SHIPPING) LTD.

CARDIFF

FUNNEL:

HOUSEFLAG:

Rudry ...	...	...	...	1946	960	219	32	10	SR(A)

M.V. Fernfield. Zillah Shpg. Co. [*Fotoship*

M.V. Wicklow. British & Irish S.P. Co. [*J. Clarkson*

WITHERINGTON & EVERETT LTD.

NEWCASTLE

FUNNEL: *Black with broad band of vertical black and white stripes.*
HOUSEFLAG: *Red with large white letters "W & E".*

CRACKSHOT STEAM SHIPPING CO.									
Chevychase ...	...	...	...	1956	902	234	36	13	M(A
GRANTA STEAM SHIPPING CO. LTD.									
Sprightly	...	...	...	1959	1,591	256	39	—	M

Eire

ALLIANCE & DUBLIN CONSUMERS GAS CO. LTD.

DUBLIN

FUNNEL: *Black with white letter "G".*
HOUSEFLAG: *Orange with company's arms in black and white.*
SERVICES: *Coal from North West coast ports to Dublin gasworks.*

Glenbride	...	...	...	...	1952	370	147	25	—	M(A)
Glencullen	...	...	...	...	1952	400	139	24	—	M(A)

Geo. BELL & CO. LTD.

DUBLIN

FUNNEL:
HOUSEFLAG:

Susan ...	...	...	...	...	1957	487	171	28	10	M(A)

BRITISH & IRISH STEAM PACKET CO. LTD.

DUBLIN

FUNNEL: *Green with black top separated by narrow white band.*

HOUSEFLAG: *White with green-edged red St. George's cross.*

SERVICES: *Dublin–Liverpool (Passenger); Dublin, Drogheda, Newry, etc., to Mersey ports (Cargo).*

Dundalk	...	...	...	...	1939	710	193	35	12	M
Inniscarra	...	...	...	...	1948	584	177	28	11	M(A)
Kilkenny	...	...	...	...	1937	1,320	276	40	12	M
Leinster	...	...	...	...	1948	4,115	367	50	17½	M(2)
Meath	...	...	...	...	1960	1,590	288	47	13	M
Munster	...	...	...	...	1948	4,142	367	50	17½	M(2)
Wicklow	...	...	...	...	1938	586	196	32	11	M(A)

CELTIC COASTERS, LTD.

CORK

FUNNEL: *Black with broad band of green and white diagonal stripes.*

HOUSEFLAG: *None.*

Coastal Tankers:

Breeda J.	...	...	...	...	1936	359	138	24	—	M(A)
Elfie H.	...	...	...	...	1943	499	162	27	—	M(A)
Jill J.	...	...	...	...	1950	677	195	29	—	M(A)
Mary D.	...	...	...	...	1940	435	158	26	—	M(A)
Renee J.	...	...	...	...	1945	284	143	21	—	M(A)

CITY OF CORK STEAM PACKET CO. LTD.
(BRITISH & IRISH S.P.CO. SUBSIDIARY)

CORK

FUNNEL: *White with black top.*

HOUSEFLAG:

SERVICES: *Cork–Fishguard (Passenger); Cork–Liverpool (Cargo).*

Glanmire	...	...	...	...	1936	814	237	37	—	M(2)
Innisfallen	...	...	...	...	1948	3,705	340	50	17	M(2)

CORAS IOMPAIR EIREANN
(IRISH TRANSPORT CO.)
DUBLIN

FUNNEL: *Red with company's winged wheel device in white between two narrow white bands.*

HOUSEFLAG: *Green with winged wheel in paler green edged with yellow.*

SERVICES: *Galway–Aran Islands (Passenger and Cargo).*

Naom Eanna	...	...	...	1953	483	137	28	—	M(A)

GREENORE FERRY SERVICES LTD.
GREENORE

FUNNEL:

HOUSEFLAG:

SERVICES:

Owenro	...	...	...	...	1965	598	214	32	—	M(A)

HALL & TYRRELL
ARKLOW

FUNNEL: *Blue with black top and houseflag.*

HOUSEFLAG: *White with blue monogram "H A".*

Kilbride	...	...	...	...	1942	321	137	25	8	M(A)
River Avoca	...	...	...	...	1948	384	144	25	9	M(A)

IRISH MOTORSHIPS, LTD.
WEXFORD

FUNNEL:

HOUSEFLAG:

Menapia	...	...	...	...	1939	1,000	214	33	10½	M(A)

M.V. Irish Willow. Irish Shpg. Ltd. *J. Clarkson*

M.V. Sand Gull. S. Coast Shpg. Co. *[D. R. Chesterton*

IRISH SHIPPING LTD.

DUBLIN

FUNNEL: *Yellow with broad green band between two narrow white bands.*

HOUSEFLAG: *White with red St. Andrew's cross and the arms of the four provinces in full colour in each quarter.*

Irish Fir	...	...	...	...	1956	1,752	259	39	12	M(A)
Irish Rose	...	...	...	...	1956	1,749	259	39	12	M(A)
Irish Willow		...	...	...	1956	1,743	259	39	12	M(A)
Coastal Tanker:									
Irish Holly	...	...	...	...	1954	2,940	330	46	11½	SR(A)

Also large Ocean Freighters.

GEORGE KEARON

ARKLOW

FUNNEL: *Green with orange letter "K" in white-edged green diamond.*

HOUSEFLAG: *As funnel.*

Gloria	...	...	...	...	1951	446	163	25	10	M(A)
Reginald Kearon		...	...	...	1957	464	164	28	10	M(A)

V. NOLAN LTD.

DUBLIN

FUNNEL:

HOUSEFLAG:

Iveragh	...	...	...	...	1936	413	—	—	—	M(A)
Loch Linnhe		...	...	...	1928	753	190	29	—	SR(A)

LIMERICK STEAMSHIP CO. LTD.

LIMERICK

FUNNEL: *Black with broad red over narrow white band.*

HOUSEFLAG: *White with red St. George's cross and the black letters "L S S Co." in each quarter.*

SERVICES: *Limerick and West Irish ports to Liverpool and to North Continental ports (Cargo).*

Derrynane	...	...	...	...	1950	470	200	30	13	M(A)
Mulcair	...	...	...	...	1958	500	194	40	—	M(A)
Oranmore	...	...	...	...	1962	472	191	30	13	M(A)
Shannon	...	...	...	...	1964	590	214	32	—	M(A)

MARINE TRANSPORT SERVICES, LTD.

COBH

FUNNEL:

HOUSEFLAG:

Mossville	...	...	...	...	1953	535	185	29	—	M(A)
Sarsfield	...	...	...	...	1956	622	203	31	—	M(A)
West Coast	...	...	...	...	1951	423	—	—	—	M(A)

Under 200 tons: **Celt, Corpach,** and **The Miller**

PALGRAVE MURPHY (SHIPPING) LTD.

DUBLIN

FUNNEL: *Yellow with green shamrock on green-edged white shield.*

HOUSEFLAG: *Divided horizontally red over white over red, with black letters "P. M. (S) Ltd." on the white.*

SERVICES: *Dublin and other Irish ports to French and Belgian ports (Cargo).*

City of Cork	...	...	...	1960	1,200	267	39	—	M(A)
City of Dublin	...	...	...	1955	970	242	36	12½	M

SHELL MEX & B.P. LTD.

CORK

FUNNEL: *Black with broad yellow band between two narrow white bands.*

HOUSEFLAG:

Coastal Tanker:									
Shell Mex 5	...	...	...	...	1921	440	152	28	—	SR(A)

TRANSMARINE INTERNATIONAL LTD.

DUBLIN

FUNNEL:

HOUSEFLAG:

Iveragh	...	...	...	...	1936	413	158	26	—	M(A)

J. TYRRELL LTD.

ARKLOW

FUNNEL: *Yellow with broad white band between two narrow green bands.*

HOUSEFLAG:

Marizell	...	...	...	...	1948	418	159	26	10	M(A)
Murell	...	...	...	...	1940	319	139	25	8	M(A)
Tyrronall	...	...	...	...	1935	248	136	23	7	M(A)
Valzell	...	...	...	...	1935	576	176	31	—	M(A)

JOHN TYRRELL

ARKLOW

FUNNEL: *Yellow with narrow black top.*

HOUSEFLAG:

Alfred Mason	...	...	...	1919	305	133	23	10	M(A)

MICHAEL G. TYRRELL

ARKLOW

FUNNEL: *Green with orange letter "T" in white triangle.*

HOUSEFLAG:

Avondale	...	...	...	...	1950	303	144	24	—	M(A)

Sand Carriers, Suction Dredgers, etc.

The following list is not exhaustive but contains the majority of the larger companies employing coasting vessels in the sand trade. Most trade only in the neighbourhood of their home ports, but some, notably the vessels of the South Coast Shipping Co. which trade between Dover and the South Devon ports, operate more widely. All are motorships except those marked by an asterisk which are steamers.

R. ABEL & SONS, LTD., Liverpool

Lunesdale*	1901	562	Peakdale*	1910	507
Monsaldale*	1879	376	Stockdale*	1888	174

ASHMEAD (PADSTOW) LTD., Padstow

Stowmead	1933	377	Westmead	1928	197

F. BOWLES & SON, Cardiff
(Also operating from the Thames)

Bowbelle	1964	1,486		Bowpride	1960	780
Bowcrest	1955	587		Bowprince	196	1,599
Bowline	1953	599		Bowstar	1950	561

THE BRISTOL SAND & GRAVEL CO. LTD., Bristol

Badminton	1956	610		Dunkerton*	1934	505
Camerton*	1950	891		Peterson	1961	749

WM. COOPER & SONS, LTD., Liverpool

Emily II*	1933	291		John L. K.*	1924	718
S. E. Copper*	1938	657		P. M. Cooper*	1925	775

THE FLEETWOOD SAND & GRAVEL CO. LTD., Fleetwood

Alladale*	1907	450

FOREMOST DREDGING CO. LTD., Southampton

Seastone*	1907	861		Wightstone*	1950	1,313

WM. FRANCE, FENWICK & CO. LTD., London

Gritwood	1963	987

HOLMS SAND & GRAVEL CO. LTD., Bristol

Harry Brown	1962	634		Portway*	1927	298
Steepholm*	1950	532				

NORWEST SAND & GRAVEL CO. LTD., Liverpool

Norstar	1961	614		Norwest	1955	596

P. E. PENFOLD LTD, Newhaven and Southampton

Pen Adur	1943	309		Pen Itchen	1947	410
Pen Arun	1943	311		Ron Woolaway	1958	478
Pen Dart	1957	499		Seaborne Alpha*	1912	410

(These vessels are operated by a number of subsidiary companies)

SAND & GRAVEL MARKETING CO. LTD., Cardiff

Sand Galore*	1935	3,145

SOUTH COAST SHIPPING CO. LTD., Southampton

Sand Diver	1944	379		Sand Runner	1943	302
Sand Grebe	1959	531		Sand Skipper	1943	313
Sand Gull	1959	534		Sand Snipe	1961	517
Sand Lark	1963	540		Sand Star	1942	488
Sand Martin	1936	633		Sand Tern	1964	535

SOUTH WALES SAND & GRAVEL CO. LTD., Swansea

Glen Gower	1963	552		Glen Hafod	1960	552

TAY SAND CO. LTD., Dundee

Edith*	1920	320		Isabel*	1915	287
Glen Helen*	1918	315				

W. WOOLAWAY & SONS, LTD., Barnstaple

Stan Woolaway	1955	278		Wm. Woolaway	1964	355

FOREIGN
COASTAL SHIPS

M.V. Venus. Bergen Line

INTRODUCTION

The ships listed in the following pages are mainly Short Sea or Coastal Passenger and Cargo Ships or Tankers in the service of some of the many foreign companies whose ships are to be seen in United Kingdom ports or those of North East Europe. Some operate on regular routes and these are indicated inasfar as they concern British ports, others are employed on the seasonal Baltic timber trades or in the fruit trades from the Mediterranean and Azores to British ports; the majority, however, work on tramping services.

In this edition the companies have been grouped together under their national flags, the titles of individual companies being arranged in alphabetical order of the *operative* name since many of them begin with such terms as "Societe Anonyme", etc. Apart from such obvious abbreviations as Cia. (Compania, etc.), Cie. (Compagnie), Nav. (Navegacion, etc.), Mar. (Maritime), and S.A. or Soc. Anon. (Societe Anonyme, etc.), others such as, A/B, A.G., A/S, D/S, GES. G.m.b.H., K.K., Maats., N.V., O/Y, Red., Reed., S.p.A., etc., are the foreign equivalents of "Shipping Company", "Limited Company", etc.

The tonnage given is the gross tonnage, while the length is the length overall, except in cases where only the registered length is available. This is some 5 to 15 ft. The speed is the service speed and not necessarily the maximum.

The funnel colours are those of the company under whose name they appear. Many Dutch and German owners manage additional ships on behalf of smaller concerns or "captain-owners", the names of these ships are included in the lists and as a consequence not all the ships listed necessarily wear the colours stated. It must also be remembered that ships may be working on charter to another company and may wear that concern's colours for the duration of the charter. Thus a particular ship may wear her own companies colours, those of her "captain-owners", or those of some quite different owner to whom she is chartered; she may even arrive at a port with one funnel design and leave with another! Where variations of this kind are most likely to occur a note referring to this introduction is given. The terms "Buff", "Cream", or "Stone Colour" have been avoided as being liable to lead to confusion, the term "Yellow" being used to cover all varieties of shade.

M.V. Diamant. S.A. Cockerill—Ougree.   [*John G. Callis*

M.V. Yvonne. Armement L. Hermanns.   [*John G. Callis*

Belgium

BELGIAN MARINE ADMINISTRATION

OSTEND

FUNNEL: *Yellow with black top.*

HOUSEFLAG: *Belgian National flag worn as ensign.*

SERVICES: *Ostend–Dover (Passenger, Car Ferry and Cargo)*

Name	Date	Tons Gross	Length (feet)	Breadth (feet)	Speed (knots)	Engines
Artevelde*	1959	2,812	383	49	21	M(2)
Ijzer	1953	1,157	219	39	15	M
Koning Albert	1948	3,701	373	47	25¼	M(2)
Koningen Elisabeth	1957	3,794	374	50	23½	M(2)
Koningen Fabiola*	1963	—	385	52	—	M(2)
Prince Philippe	1948	3,701	372	47	25¼	M(2)
Prins Albert	1937	2,994	372	47	25¼	M(2)
Prinses Josephine-Charlotte* ...	1949	2,537	373	52	22	M(2)
Reine Astrid	1958	3,794	374	50	23½	M(2)
Roi Baudouin	1934	3,120	372	47	25¼	M(2)
Roi Leopold III	1956	3,794	374	50	23½	M(2)

Also tugs and salvage craft at Ostend.   *Car Ferries

SOC. ANON. COCKERILL-OUGREE

ANTWERP

FUNNEL: *Yellow with black top.*

HOUSEFLAG: *Belgian National flag with company's device in black on the yellow stripe and white letters "C O" on red and black.*

SERVICES: *Antwerp–Tilbury, Ostend–Tilbury (Cargo)*

Diamant	1953	548	176	26	11	M(A)
Rubis	1957	574	183	27	13	M(A)
Saphir	1954	553	173	26	12½	M(A)
Topaze	1954	560	179	26	12½	M(A)
Turquoise	1958	574	183	27	13	M(A)

M.V. Marguerite. Armement L. Hermanns. [*John Mannering*

M.V. Castor. Soc. Belge 'Navibel' S.A. [*John G. Callis*

ARMEMENT L. HERMANNS, S.A.

ANTWERP

FUNNEL: *Black with large white letter "H" on broad red band.*

HOUSEFLAG: *Red with large white letter "H"*

Alfonso	...	...	...	...	1950	1,335	231*	37	14	M(A)
Charles	...	...	...	...	1949	1,180	231*	37	14	M(A)
Marcel	...	...	...	...	1939	557	177*	29	12	M(A)
Marguerite	...	...	...	...	1943	1,837	290*	44	12	M
Maria	...	...	...	...	1959	988	270*	38	—	M(A)
Rene	...	...	...	...	1952	1,346	232*	37	15	M(A)
Rosa	...	...	...	...	1945	1,346	247*	36	14	M(A)
Santiago	...	...	...	...	1954	1,300	247*	36	—	M(A)
Yvonne	...	...	...	...	1949	1,187	231*	37	14	M(A)

REEDERIJ JANSEGERS

ANTWERP

FUNNEL:

HOUSEFLAG:

Christian	...	...	423	Cobeltra	...	...	429	Hilda	...	...	...	429

N.V. REED. R. LEYSEN & CO.

ANTWERP

FUNNEL:

HOUSEFLAG:

Frank L.	...	...	485	Peter L.	...	...	485	Roland	...	...	466

SOC. BELGE DE NAV. MARITIME "NAVIBEL"

ANTWERP

FUNNEL: *Red with narrow black top and red "N B" monogram on broad yellow band.*

HOUSEFLAG: *Red with red "N B" monogram on broad diagonal yellow band from bottom of hoist.*

Castor	...	...	...	...	1954	1,035	232	35	12½	M(A)
Jason	...	...	...	...	1957	1,052	232	35	13	M(A)
Pollux	...	...	...	...	1954	1,035	232	35	12¾	M(A)
Thesee	...	...	...	...	1964	1,585	274	39	—	M(A)

M.V. Artevelde. Belgian State Marine. [*John G. Callis*

M.V. Konigen Fabiola. Belgian State Marine. [*John Mannering*

Denmark

C. CLAUSEN'S D/S A/S

COPENHAGEN

FUNNEL: *Black with blue band between two white bands.*
HOUSEFLAG: *Blue with blue letter "C" on white diamond.*

Clara Clausen	...	...	...	1963	1,959	328	49	10	M(A)
Dona Clausen	...	...	...	1965	2,750	326	48	—	M(A)
Helene Clausen	...	...	...	1955	300	157	28	11	M(A)
Ida Clausen ...	...	...	...	1957	299	156	29	—	M(A)
Ilse Clausen ...	...	...	...	1958	299	156	29	—	M(A)
Inger Clausen	...	...	...	1957	299	156	29	—	M(A)
Irene Clausen	...	...	...	1958	299	156	29	—	M(A)
Iris Clausen ...	...	...	...	1959	299	156	29	—	M(A)

RED. OTTO DANIELSEN

COPENHAGEN

FUNNEL: *Green with large letters "O D", some with narrow black top.*
HOUSEFLAG: *Green with large white letters "O D".*

Anne Bogelund	...	...	...	1962	1,503	264	39	—	M(A)
Ellen Helleskov	...	...	...	1961	499	200	30	—	M(A)
Embla ...	...	...	...	1962	299	158	28	—	M(A)
Eny Hojsgaard	...	...	...	1962	1,384	241	38	—	M(A)
Etly Danielsen	...	...	...	1959	1,562	282	39	12¾	M(A)
Gitte Ginge ...	...	...	...	1963	1,255	252	37	—	M(A)
H. I. Kroyre ...	...	...	...	1962	299	158	28	—	M(A)
John Helleskov	...	...	...	1966	1,260	—	—	—	M(A)
Ketty Danielsen	...	...	...	1963	1,399	264	39	12	M(A)
Marie Helleskov	...	...	...	1964	1,274	241	39	—	M(A)
Nete Ginge ...	...	...	...	1963	1,255	252	37	—	M(A)
Thea Danielsen	...	...	...	1962	1,483	269	39	—	M(A)

NIELSEN & BRESLING RED.

COPENHAGEN

FUNNEL:
HOUSEFLAG:

Single-screw Motorships with engines aft

Astrid Bres ...	...	399	Elise Bres	...	...	300	Lone Bres	...	...	399
Cynthia Bres	...	300	Jytte Bres	...	...	299				

D/S A/S PROGRESS
O. AMSINCK
COPENHAGEN

FUNNEL: *Black with red seven-pointed star on broad white band.*

HOUSEFLAG:

Aase Nielsen	...	...	...	1958	3,193	344	48	—	M
Anna Nielsen	...	...	...	1958	1,198	275	40	—	M(A)
Ellen Nielsen	...	...	...	1949	1,584	285	41	12½	M
Grete Nielsen	...	...	...	1960	1,281	267	41	—	M(A)
Hugo Nielsen	...	...	...	1949	1,594	285	41	12½	M(A)
Marius Nielsen	...	...	...	1954	1,600	284	41	12	M
Rigmor Nielsen	...	...	...	1954	1,600	282	41	12	M

A. E. SORENSEN
SVENDBORG

FUNNEL: *Yellow with narrow black top and swallow-tail houseflag on broad blue band.*

HOUSEFLAG: *White swallowtail with red border at top and bottom and blue letters "A E S" in centre.*

A. E. S.	...	...	...	...	1957	994	257	37	—	M(A)
Elin S.	...	...	...	...	1949	500	158	29	—	M(A)
Louis S.	...	...	...	...	1961	400	166	27	—	M
Martin S.	...	...	...	...	1963	2,315	290	42	11½	M(A)
Nancie S.	...	...	...	...	1953	500	212	32	—	M(A)
Nanok S.	...	...	...	...	1961	2,232	290	42	—	M(A)
Patricia S.	...	...	...	...	1961	400	167	27	—	M(A)
Peder Most	...	...	...	...	1961	399	167	27	—	M(A)
Procyon	...	...	...	...	1938	365	147	25	—	M(A)
Renate S.	...	...	...	...	1957	399	163	27	—	M(A)
Sigrid S.	...	...	...	...	1949	499	160	29	—	M(A)

UNITED STEAMSHIP CO.
(DET FORENEDE DAMPSKIBS-SELSKAB A/B—D.F.D.S.)
COPENHAGEN

FUNNEL: *Black with broad red band.*

HOUSEFLAG: *Blue with large white Maltese cross.*

SERVICES: *Esjberg–Harwich, Esjberg–Newcastle, Esjberg–London (Passenger). Danish ports to London, Newcastle, Leith, Middlesbrough, Hull, Grimsby, Newport, Liverpool, Manchester, etc. (Cargo). Other services to European, North African and American ports.*

Andros	...	...	...	...	1954	1,810	331	45	15	M
Athos ...	...	...	...	...	1961	2,660	362	51	—	M
Bangsbo	...	...	...	...	1952	1,866	303	44	13	M
Bellona	...	...	...	...	1955	1,481	292	42	14½	M

M.V. Blenda. Det Forenede Dampskibs. *[Fotoship*

M.V. Knudsholm. Det Forenede Dampskibs. *[Fotoship*

Bergenhus	...	...	...	...	1964	780	—	—	10	M
Blenda	...	...	...	...	1956	1,481	293	42	13½	M
Borreby	...	...	...	...	1953	1,875	303	44	13	M
Broager	...	...	...	...	1953	1,875	303	44	13	M
Diana ...	...	...	...	...	1945	1,082	262	36	11½	SR
Egholm	...	...	...	...	1944	1,752	301	44	9½	SR
England	...	...	...	...	1964	8,221	459	63	—	M
Ficaria	...	...	...	...	1951	1,811	332	46	14½	M
Freesia	...	...	...	...	1961	2,683	362	51	15½	M
Katholm	...	...	...	...	1961	684	241	34	11½	M(A)
Klausholm	...	...	...	...	1958	694	241	34	11½	M(A)
Klintholm	...	...	...	...	1950	695	219	33	10	M(A)
Knudsholm	...	...	...	...	1959	699	241	34	11½	M(A)
Kongsholm	...	...	...	...	1963	1,150	241	34	11½	M(A)
Korsholm	...	...	...	...	1950	965	219	33	10	M(A)
Kronholm	...	...	...	...	1962	1,150	241	34	11½	M(A)
Kronprins Frederik	...	...	...	1941	3,937	376	50	20½	M(2)
Kronprinsesse Ingrid	...	...	...	1936	3,968	376	50	20½	M(2)
Kyholm	...	...	...	...	1961	688	241	34	11½	M(A)
Magnolia	...	...	...	...	1962	2,359	350	50	—	M
Marocco	...	...	...	...	1936	1,684	288	40	11½	M
Petunia	...	...	...	...	1962	2,383	350	50	—	M
Primula	...	...	...	...	1952	1,812	331	46	14½	M
Tunis ...	...	...	...	...	1936	1,690	288	40	11½	M

Other ships include: **Aalborghus, Axelhus, Bastholm, Birkholm, Botnia, Bygholm, C. F. Tietgen, Dronning Alexandrine, Egholm, Hans Broge, H. P. Prior, Jens Bang, King Olav V, Lemnos, Melos, Naxos, Prinsesse Margarethe, Rhodos, Riberhus, Samos, Skyrog** and **Vistula.** Also larger Ocean Freighters.

Finland

ETELA-SUOMEN LAIVA O/Y

HELSINGFORS

FUNNEL: *Black with two narrow white bands crossed in the centre of each side to form an "X".*

HOUSEFLAG: *Black with two white bands as on funnel.*

Arkadia	...	...	...	...	1943	2,664	321	46	10	SR
Espa ...	...	...	...	...	1948	2,226	351	51	11	SR
Hakaniemi	...	...	...	...	1949	2,273	330	47	—	SR
Kaisaniemi	...	...	...	...	1940	1,989	318	43	12	RT

O/Y FINNLINES, LTD.

HELSINGFORS

FUNNEL: *Black with black letter "F" in white circle interrupting blue band between two white bands.*

HOUSEFLAG: *Blue over white with blue letter "F" on white disc.*

Finnbirch	...	...	...	...	1953	2,731	369	48	13½	M(A)
Finnfighter	...	...	...	...	1964	1,735	318	46	—	M(A)
Finnpine	...	...	...	...	1958	1,318	258	41	—	M(A)
Finnwood	...	...	...	...	1956	1,185	275	40	12	M(A)

M.V. Poseidon. Finska Angfartygs A/B. [*Fotoship*

M.V. Titania. Finska Angfartygs A/B. [*Fotoship*

MERIVIENTI O/Y

Finnalpino	...	...	...	...	1958	2,883	375	50	—	M(A)
Finnkraft	...	...	...	...	1956	1,990	321	46	13	M(A)
Finnstar	...	...	...	...	1955	2,914	370	50	13½	M(A)
Hansa Express		...	...	...	1962	2,977	315	52	—	M(A)

Also larger Ocean Freighters.

FINSKA ANGFARTYGS A/B
HELSINKI

FUNNEL: *Black with two white rings.*

HOUSEFLAG: *Blue over white over blue, with blue letters "F A A" on white.*

SERVICES: *Finland to London and Hull (Passenger and Cargo). Finland to various British ports (Cargo). Also services to Northern Europe, the Mediterranean, New York and South America.*

Aldebaran	...	...	...	...	1938	1,957	310	41	11	SR
Arcturus	...	...	...	...	1960	1,472	293	43	13½	M(A)
Argo ...	...	...	...	...	1963	2,673	382	53	—	M
Astraea	...	...	...	...	1956	1,519	307	44	15	M
Capella	...	...	...	...	1945	1,555	274	39	11	SR
Castor...	...	...	...	...	1962	1,471	293	43	—	M(A)
Ceres ...	...	...	...	...	1952	1,347	249	37	11	M(A)
Clio ...	...	...	...	...	1944	1,561	274	39	11	SR
Fennia	...	...	...	...	1944	1,488	279	34	11	SR
Finlandia	...	...	...	...	1946	2,163	296	43	10	SR
Hebe ...	...	...	...	...	1962	2,269	293	43	—	M(A)
Juno ...	...	...	...	...	1948	1,923	304	44	11½	SR
Leo ...	...	...	...	...	1948	1,923	304	44	11½	SR
Mira ...	...	...	...	...	1956	1,378	292	42	13½	M(A)
Pallas ...	...	...	...	...	1953	2,218	315	44	13	SR
Patria ...	...	...	...	...	1947	2,162	297	43	10	SR
Polaris	...	...	...	...	1956	1,519	307	44	13	M
Pollux	...	...	...	...	1959	1,326	258	41	—	M
Poseidon	...	...	...	...	1957	1,400	292	42	13½	M(A)
Salla ...	...	...	...	...	1957	1,374	292	42	13½	M(A)
Taurus	...	...	...	...	1960	1,422	292	42	13½	M(A)
Tellus ...	...	...	...	...	1960	1,422	292	42	13	M(A)
Titania	...	...	...	...	1961	1,422	292	42	13	M(A)
Triton	...	...	...	...	1961	1,422	292	42	13	M(A)
Vega ...	...	...	...	...	1957	1,372	292	42	13	M(A)

Other ships include: **Aallotar, Antares, Alli, Ara, Ariadne, Ariel, Baltic, Bjarmia, Carelia, Corona, Dione, Frej, Heros, Hektos, Hesperus, Ilamtar, Inari, Inba, Inio, Iris, Ivalo, Kurki, Lapponia, Leda, Lokki, Norma, Oihanna, Orion, Pohjanmaa, Regulus, Rhea, Rigel, Sirius, Sotka, Vesta, Vikla, Virgo** and **Wellamo.**

ALGOT JOHANSSON
MARIEHAMM

FUNNEL: *Black with blue band between two white bands.*

HOUSEFLAG: *Blue with white border at top and bottom and the yellow letters "A. J." in the centre.*

Dagny	...	...	...	...	1927	1,734	295	42	12	SR
Helny ...	...	...	...	...	1959	498	220	32	13	M(A)
Panny ...	...	...	...	...	1942	716	203	30	9	M(A)

Also larger Ocean Freighters.

M.V. Finnpine. O/Y Finnlines. [*John G. Callis*

S.S. Kari Ragnar. A/B R. Nordstrom. [*J. Clarkson*

A/B R. NORDSTROM & CO. O/Y

LOVISA

FUNNEL: *Black or yellow with black letter "N" on white diamond on red over green band.*

HOUSEFLAG: *Black letter "N" on white diamond on red over green horizontal bands.*

Annika	...	...	...	...	1965	1,809	—	—	—	M(A)
Kari Ragnar	...	...	...	...	1927	2,472	341	46	—	SR
Kenneth	...	...	...	...	1939	1,880	300	44	10	RT
Kristina	...	...	...	...	1951	1,370	258	42	10½	RT
Nina	...	...	...	...	1963	2,363	307	45	—	M(A)
Peter	...	...	...	...	1948	2,340	335	47	—	SR

Also larger Ocean Freighters.

RAUMANMERI O/Y
E. FAGERSTROM

RAUMA

FUNNEL: *Black with yellow device on broad blue band over narrow white band.*

HOUSEFLAG:

Hakuni	...	...	...	...	1927	1,804	279	42	—	SR
Petajas	...	...	...	...	1934	1,598	254	40	—	SR

France

AGENCE MARITIME DE L'OUEST

BORDEAUX

FUNNEL:

HOUSEFLAG:

All single-screw vessels with engines aft

L'Armoricain	...	498	La Paimpolaise	...	455	La Trieux	...	...	500
Le Leonard	...	...	377	Le Tregor	...	...	255	Stella Matutina	...	292

ANGLETERRE-LORRAINE-ALSACE S. A. DE NAV.

DUNKIRK

See British Railways (Southern Region)

SOC. NAVALE CAENNAISE

CAEN

FUNNEL: *Black with broad red band containing the white letters "S N C" between two narrow white bands.*

HOUSEFLAG: *Divided horizontally white over red over white, with white letters "S N C" on red band.*

Amalthee	...	...	...	...	1961	3,122	325	47	—	M(A)
Astree...	...	...	...	...	1954	3,074	329	47	—	M(A)
Boree ...	...	...	...	...	1961	2,059	297	44	—	M(A)
Circe ...	...	...	...	...	1958	2,874	281	41	17	M
Danae	...	...	...	...	1936	2,660	322	44	—	SR
Daphne	...	...	...	...	1947	1,997	295	40	10	SR
Dione ...	...	...	...	...	1947	2,613	323	44	10	SR
Enee ...	...	...	...	...	1956	1,332	263	29	15	M
Francoise le Brise	...	...	...	1957	2,343	278	44	11	M
Nelee ...	...	...	...	...	1958	2,874	281	41	17	M(A)
Neree	...	...	...	...	1954	2,174	267	44	—	M(A)
Neve ...	...	...	...	...	1961	852	248	36	—	M(A)
Niobe	...	...	...	...	1946	2,010	296	40	10	SR
Noe* ...	...	...	...	...	1963	2,603	298	44	—	M(A)
Orphee	...	...	...	...	1952	1,379	272	39	12½	M(A)
Phebe ...	...	...	...	...	1956	2,343	278	44	—	M(A)
Phryne	...	...	...	...	1948	2,159	299	46	—	M(A)
Psyche...	...	...	...	...	1952	1,795	264	39	12	SR
Typhee	...	...	...	...	1958	2,405	285	44	—	M

Also larger Ocean Freighters.
*Wine Tanker.

CITERNA MARITIME S.A.

PARIS

FUNNEL: *Black with white letter "C" on blue over red bands.*

HOUSEFLAG: *Blue over red with large white letter "C".*

Coastal Tankers:

Alize ...	...	...	...	...	1928	2,637	313	50	—	M(A)
Eole ...	...	...	...	...	1958	1,422	251	37	11½	M(A)
Eurus ...	...	...	...	...	1958	944	217	31	—	M(A)
Noroit	...	...	...	...	1954	1,839	267	38	9	M(A)
Sudest	...	...	...	...	1939	793	208	29	9½	M(A)
Zephyr	...	...	...	...	1954	1,153	219	35	11	M(A)

S.S. Dione. Soc. Nav. Caennaise. [*John G. Callis*

M.V. Suderau. Bugsier Reederei. [*John G. Callis*

M.V. Ortrud Muller. Otto A. Muller. Since withdrawn [*John G. Callis*

CIE. CHARLES LE BORGNE

PARIS

FUNNEL: *Black with white letters "C L B" on blue star in red bordered white diamond on narrow red and white rings between two blue rings.*

HOUSEFLAG: *Narrow red and white horizontal stripes. Blue five-pointed star containing the white letters "C L B" in centre.*

Augustin le Borgne	...	...	1956	1,318	284	38	14¾	M(A)
Charles le Borgne ...	...	...	1948	2,149	300	46	14	M
Marie-Agnes le Borgne	...	...	1951	958	243	40	13	M
Marie-Louise le Borgne	...	...	1956	1,293	284	38	14¾	M(A)
Marie-Therese le Borgne	...	...	1962	1,599	278	43	—	M(2A)
Pierre le Borgne	...	...	1951	985	243	40	13	M

Also larger Ocean Freighters.

S. N. C. F. FRENCH RAILWAYS

CALAIS

See under British Railways

TRANSPORTS MARITIMES DE SUD-OUEST
G. GARROUSTE

PESSAC-GIRONDE

FUNNEL:

HOUSEFLAG:

All single-screw Motor vessels										
Blancpigeon ...	...	498	**Bounty**	...	...	500	**Guyenne**	...	...	500

WORMS & CIE.

PARIS

FUNNEL: *Black.*

HOUSEFLAG: *Blue with large white disc at centre.*

Chateau Lafitte	...	...	...	1958	2,360	293	39	—	SR
Chateau Margaux	...	...	...	1958	2,375	334	47	14½	M(A)
Chateau Yquem	...	...	...	1952	1,488	292	42	12½	M(A)
Leoville	...	...	...	...	1959	1,204	284	38	15½	M(2A)
Normanville	...	...	...	1957	2,624	320	44	12	M(2A)
Pomerol	...	...	...	1957	1,208	285	38	15	M(A)
Yainville	...	...	...	1961	2,662	317	44	—	M(2A)

Germany

(East German Democratic Republic)

DEUTSCHE SEEREEDEREI

ROSTOCK

FUNNEL: *Yellow with narrow black top and broad red band between two narrow blue bands.*

HOUSEFLAG: *Divided horizontally blue over red over blue, with white letters "D S R" on the red.*

(The Deutsche Seereederei is the State-controlled shipping organization of the Democratic Republic and almost all the vessels listed are contained in three standard classes, all single-screw motorships with engines aft).

Ahrenshoop ...	...	432	Graal-Muritz	...	432	Sassnitz ...	...	430
Albatros ...	...	980	Griefswald ...	...	434	Sirrah ...	...	617
Aldebaran ...	...	617	Heringsdorf ...	...	439	Stavenhagen ...	...	586
Anklam ...	...	430	Insel Reims ...	...	617	Stoltera ...	...	1,831
Arcturus ...	...	617	Kormoran ...	...	983	Stubbenkammer	...	1,814
Atair ...	...	617	Koserow ...	...	432	Timmendorf ...	...	432
Barhoft ...	...	432	Kuhlungsborn	...	432	Uckermunde	...	617
Bellatrix ...	...	617	Markab ...	...	617	Vilm ...	...	617
Bussard ...	...	983	Nordstern ...	...	617	Vitte ...	...	617
Capella ...	...	617	Ostseebad Wustrow	...	430	Waren ...	...	617
Condor ...	...	983	Peenemunde	...	432	Warnemunde	...	430
Deneb ...	...	617	Poel ...	...	617	Wega ...	...	617
Denebola ...	...	617	Prerow ...	...	432	Wolgast ...	...	430
Falke ...	...	983	Putbus ...	...	617	Zingst ...	...	432
Flamingo ...	...	983	Rerik ...	...	617	Zinnowitz ...	...	617
Gemma ...	...	617	Rositz ...	...	791			

Germany

(West German Federal Republic)

KUSTENSCHIFFAHRT BAUER & HAUSCHILDT K.G.

HAMBURG

FUNNEL: *See introductory note.*

HOUSEFLAG:

All single-screw motorships with engines aft

Alma II ...	...	281	Dithmarschen	...	378	Esteland ...	...	499
Anita Schutt...	...	365	Edelgard ...	...	293	Gertrud ...	...	299
Anne-Luise Wupper		484	Egon Wesch ...	...	499	Gesa Meinken	...	400
Basbeck ...	...	423	Elbstrom ...	...	424	Gisela	...	286
Bernd Becker	...	423	Esdorp ...	...	225	Hanna Dreier	...	388
Bernd-Gunda	...	387	Este ...	...	422	Hannes Lundstedt	...	424
Bewa	...	425	Estebrugge ...	...	499	Hans Bulow ...	...	423
Cherie... ...	...	212	Esteburg ...	...	500	Hedwig Lundstedt	...	424

M.V. Hille Oldendorff. Egon Oldendorff.   [*John G. Callis*

M.V. Cressida. A. Kirsten & Co.   [*J. Clarkson*

Heimwarts	...	...	249	Julius Hauschildt	...	424	Martha Nibbe	...	422
Heinrich Hauschildt		425	Jupiter	...	...	407	Nordkap	...	424
Helga Brohan	...	281	Jurger Stahmer	...	422	Oste	...	...	417
Helga Hauschildt	...	425	Kathe Ahrens	...	425	Otma	...	...	271
Hella	...	...	399	Kathe Bartels	...	498	Peter S	...	299
Hera	...	...	425	Kathe Jonas	...	497	Planet	...	...	499
Hildegarde Bulow	...	424	Kathe-Marie	...	413	Peter Meyer	...	294
Ilse Wolter	...	422	Kathe Ritscher	...	281	Ruth	...	...	292
Inka Ritscher	...	297	Komet	...	425	Stadeland	...	421
J. H. Jonas	...	423	Konigsberg	...	200	Urania	...	219
Jans Jonas	...	425	Krautsand	...	417	Ursula Block	...	500
Jacob Becker	...	424	Leopard	...	340	Walter Behrens	...	274
Jens	...	...	299	Luhe	...	...	418	Wilhelmine		
Johannes L	...	489	Marschenland	...	298	Oltmann	...	...	372
Jonny Jonas	...	499	Martha Ahrens	...	247			

AUGUST BOLTEN
WM. MILLERS' NACHFOLDER
HAMBURG

FUNNEL: *Black with houseflag in form of broad band.*

HOUSEFLAG: *White with red border and red St. Andrew's cross and with black letter "B" in black ring superimposed on centre.*

Beate Bolten	...	...	...	1951	2,603	366	49	12½	M
Caldas	...	...	...	1953	1,743	259	41	—	M(A)
Cadiz	...	...	...	1955	2,900	392	51	—	M(2)
Scheersberg	...	...	...	1955	1,192	257	40	12½	M(A)

BRINK & WOLFSEL

FUNNEL: *See introductory note.*

HOUSEFLAG:

All single-screw motorships with engines aft

Anglia	...	...	615	Maria Althoff	...	999	Rugia	...	...	497
Heike Schluter	...	425	Merkur	...	...	400	Schleswig-Holstein	...	499
Liselotte	...	...	489	Pommern	...	...	421	Stadt Rendsberg	...	499

BUGSIER REEDEREI UND BERGUNGS A.G.
HAMBURG

FUNNEL: *Black with broad white band.*

HOUSEFLAG: *Quartered diagonally red over white over blue, and with letters "B R B A" in each quarter. (White letters on red and blue, blue letters on white).*

Finkenau	...	...	...	1961	1,197	271	—	12½	M
Holstenau	...	...	...	1961	1,214	269	36	12	M(A)
Levensau	...	...	...	1950	1,110	246	34	12½	M(2)
Norderau	...	...	...	1952	1,495	277	42	12½	M(2)
Suderau	...	...	...	1952	1,495	276	39	12½	M(2A)
Wiedau	...	...	...	1954	1,866	280	40	12	M(2)

Also a large fleet of tugs.

PETER DOHLE

HAMBURG

FUNNEL: *Black with letters "P D" on white diamond on broad red band between two narrow white bands. (See introductory note).*

HOUSEFLAG:

Adele Hagenah	...	294	Ernst de Buhr	...	425
Andrea	... ...	480	Ernst Friesecke	...	498
Andrea Luhmann	...	227	Frauke	... ...	499
Angeln	... ...	488	Freiheit	... ...	198
Annegret	... ...	423	Freida Buss	... ...	499
Annemarie Palm	...	243	Freisland	... ...	384
Antke Oltmann	...	287	Freya ...	... ...	499
Ariadne	... ...	211	Germane	... ...	368
Butt ...	... ...	421	Gert Seyd	... ...	496
Capella	... ...	497	Gretchen von		
Carina ..	... ...	424	Allworden	... ...	389
Claudia	... ...	499	Hans Oltmann	...	497
Claus ...	... ...	425	Hanse I	... ...	297
Diana ...	... ...	499	Hein Oltmann	...	333
Dini Lutter	... ...	299	Hedwig Pannbacker		353
Eggebek	... ...	499	Helga Wehr ...	...	350
Elke ...	... ...	481	Helmuth	... ...	139
Erik Seyd II	...	497	Hille ...	... ...	211
Erna Liebisch	...	299	Jacobus	... ...	231

Johanne		424
Jurgen Wehr	...	498
Kate Oltmann	...	249
Lise Oltmann	...	144
Martha Friesecke	...	499
Monica	... ...	359
Nautica	... ...	498
Neidermehnen	...	494
Nordmark	... ...	282
Palmyra	... ...	240
Ronald	... ...	293
Sagitta...	... ...	499
Sondith	... ...	297
Steinburg	... ...	499
Stormann	... ...	499
Ute ...	... ...	493
Wagrein	... ...	474
Waltraud Behrmann		422
Wiking	... ...	499

JOHN T. ESSBERGER

HAMBURG

FUNNEL: *Black with blue letter "E" on broad white band.*

HOUSEFLAG: *White with large blue letter "E".*

Coastal Tankers:								
Eduard Essberger ...	...	...	1958	624	193	28	10½	M(A)
Heinrich Essberger	...	...	1964	993	212	34	11	M(A)
Roland Essberger ...	...	...	1961	712	186	30	11	M(A)

FAIRPLAY SCHLEPPDAMPFSCH. RED.

R. BORCHARD G.m.b.H.

HAMBURG

FUNNEL: *Black with blue and red star on broad white band.*

HOUSEFLAG: *White with four-pointed blue star over four-pointed red star.*

Fairway	...	...	...	...	1953	1,406	224	36	12	M(A)
Fairwind	...	...	...	...	1956	1,778	291	44	—	M(A)

Also a fleet of tugs.

M.V. Gisela Essberger. John T. Essberger.   [*John G. Callis*

M.V. Falke. Argo Linie   [*John G. Callis*

H. M. GEHRCKENS

HAMBURG

FUNNEL: *Yellow with narrow black top.*

HOUSEFLAG: *Dark blue with large white letters "H. M. G."*

Baumwell	...	...	...	...	1951	996	269	38	12	M(A)
Bleichen	...	...	...	...	1958	1,405	306	41	12	M(A)
Borgesch	...	...	...	...	1958	1,322	306	40	12	M
Brook ...	...	...	...	...	1949	1,489	287	43	12	SR
Burstah	...	...	...	...	1955	1,322	281	40	12	ME(A
Cremon	...	...	...	...	1964	1,600	308	43	—	M(A)
Huxter	...	...	...	...	1954	745	217	34	—	M(A)
Ness ...	...	...	...	...	1955	949	251	37	12	ME(A)
Pickhuben	...	...	...	...	1953	746	217	34	12	M(A)
Plan ...	...	...	...	...	1957	291	173	30	10½	M(A)
Steckelhorn	...	...	...	...	1952	2,526	349	49	14	M
Steinhoft	...	...	...	...	1959	4,859	392	52	—	M(2A)
Stintfang	...	...	...	...	1942	2,697	341	50	14	M
Stubbenhuk	...	...	...	...	1955	2,667	356	49	14	M

CARL W. HANSSEN TANKSCHIFFAHRT

HAMBURG–BLANKENESE

FUNNEL: *Yellow with blue letter "H" interrupting broad blue band between two narrow white bands.*

HOUSEFLAG: *Divided vertically blue, white and blue, with large blue letter "H" on white.*

Coastal Tankers:

Amrun	...	...	...	...	1931	1,189	227	36	9	M(A)
Fehmarn	...	...	...	...	1929	433	139	27	7	M(A)
Nordstrand	...	...	...	...	1954	806	200	31	—	M(A)
Peleworm	...	...	...	...	1953	890	211	33	—	M
Poel ...	...	...	...	...	1942	227	131	21	9½	M
Rugen ...	...	...	...	...	1941	852	205	32	12	M(A)
Ruhrland	...	...	...	...	1954	833	200	31	—	M(A)
Sonderburg	...	...	...	...	1909	248	110	24	—	M(A)
Speikeroog	...	...	...	...	1964	994	342	37	—	M(A)
Sylt ...	...	...	...	...	1934	678	176	28	8	M
Usedom	...	...	...	...	1958	355	171	28	—	M(A)
Wangeroog	...	...	...	...	1963	1,000	240	37	—	M(A)
Wollin	...	...	...	...	1960	492	184	28	—	M(A)

A. F. HARMSTORF & CO.

HAMBURG–ALTONA

FUNNEL: *Yellow with white letter "H" on broad blue band between two narrow white bands.*

HOUSEFLAG: *Blue with broad white border at top and bottom and large white letter "H" in centre.*

Coastal Tankers:

Dieksand	...	...	...	...	1957	662	206	29	11	M(A)
Holmsand	...	...	...	...	1964	499	203	33	—	M(A)

Krautsand	...	...	...	...	1944	700	196	30	10½	M(A)
Nessand	...	...	...	...	1956	654	206	29	10½	M(A)
Guldensand	...	...	...	...	1961	1,485	266	37	—	M(A)
Rotersand	...	...	...	...	1954	2,104	282	45	14	M(A)
Rungholtsand		...	...	...	1961	892	269	39	—	M(A)
Yorksand	...	...	...	...	1964	500	203	33	—	M(A)

HEINRICH C. HORN

HAMBURG

FUNNEL: *White with white letter "H" on broad red band between two narrow blue bands.*

HOUSEFLAG: *Red with broad blue border at top and bottom and white letter "H" in centre.*

Claus Horn	...	...	...	...	1958	618	217	33	—	M(A)
Dora Horn	...	...	...	...	1958	428	196	30	—	M(A)
Heinz Horn	...	...	...	...	1958	696	232	33	—	M(A)
Herbert Horn	...	...	...	...	1959	499	207	30	—	M(A)
Hilde Horn	...	...	...	...	1959	1,137	230	33	—	M(A)
Ingrid Horn	...	...	...	...	1958	561	197	32	—	M(A)
Irmgard Horn	...	...	...	...	1959	497	207	30	—	M(A)
Luise Horn	...	...	...	...	1961	887	246	35	—	M(A)
Marie Horn	...	...	...	...	1958	696	232	33	—	M(A)
Mimi Horn	...	...	...	...	1957	389	186	29	—	M(A)
Stadt Schleswig	...	...	...	1958	428	196	30	—	M(A)
Ursula Horn	...	...	...	...	1959	1,562	246	35	—	M(A)
Waldtraut Horn	...	...	...	1958	1,022	217	33	—	M(A)

JOHANNES ICK

HAMBURG

FUNNEL: *Black with black letters "J I" on white quarters of red and white triangulated band or panel.*

HOUSEFLAG: *As funnel band.*

Rehhorst	...	...	...	...	1930	1,299	255	37	9½	SR
Uhlenhorst	...	...	...	...	1934	889	183	34	8½	M(A)

S.S. Auriga. Argo Linie. *[John G. Callis*

M.V. Trito. Hudig & Veder N.V. *[John G. Callis*

A. KIRSTEN & CO.

HAMBURG

FUNNEL: *Black.*

HOUSEFLAG: *Vertically striped red and white pennant.*

CARGO SERVICE: *Hamburg–London.*

Cressida	...	...	...	...	1954	763	218	34	11	M(A)
Emilia	...	...	...	...	1958	299	161	26	10	M(2A)
Julia ...	...	...	...	...	1957	299	161	26	10	M(2A)
Ophelia	...	...	...	...	1952	2,204	258	41	11	M(A)
Virgilia	...	...	...	...	1957	2,374	349	50	14¼	M

HAMBURG - LONDON LINE

Mariana	...	...	...	...	1954	299	161	26	10	M(2A)
Miranda	...	...	...	...	1956	299	156	26	10	M(2A)
Nerissa	...	...	...	...	1953	766	218	34	11½	M(A)
Paulina	...	...	...	...	1954	299	161	26	10	M(2A)
Tamora	...	...	...	...	1956	299	161	26	10	M(A)
Timandra	...	...	...	...	1951	499	197	31	11½	M(A)
Titania	...	...	...	...	1951	499	197	31	11½	M(2A)

KNOHR & BURCHARD, NFL.

HAMBURG

FUNNEL: *Black with blue disc on broad white band.*

HOUSEFLAG: *White with blue disc.*

Dalbek	...	...	...	...	1955	2,904	383	54	—	M
Eilbek	...	...	...	...	1956	3,904	359	49	—	RT
Ellerbek	...	...	...	...	1953	1,091	320	45	12	RT
Fischbek	...	...	...	...	1957	3,962	365	49	13½	M
Flottbek	...	...	...	...	1951	2,430	349	49	13	M
Gronnebek	...	...	...	...	1954	2,485	358	49	12	RT
Lasbek	...	...	...	...	1957	2,537	359	49	12½	RT
Rodenbek	...	...	...	...	1953	2,336	349	49	13¼	M
Schurbek	...	...	...	...	1953	2,502	358	49	12	SR
Schwarzenbek	...	...	...	...	1958	3,953	—	49	13½	M
Tarpenbek	...	...	...	...	1954	2,488	348	49	12	SR
Wandsbek	...	...	...	...	1958	3,954	365	49	13½	H

ERNST KOMROWSKI REED.

HAMBURG

FUNNEL: *Black with houseflag in form of broad band.*

HOUSEFLAG: *Quartered diagonally blue over red over blue, with white diamond superimposed on centre.*

Heluan	...	...	...	...	1951	1,544	270	39	11	M

Also larger Ocean Freighters.

HANS KRUGER, G.m.b.H.

HAMBURG

FUNNEL: *Yellow with narrow black top and black letters "H K" on black bordered white diamond.*

HOUSEFLAG: *White with deep blue border at top and bottom and black letters "H K" in centre.*

Braunsfeld	...	...	...	...	1956	1,231	226	37	11¾	M(A)
Clio ...	...	...	...	...	1959	3,126	321	47	13½	M(A)
Ehrenfeld	...	...	...	...	1951	1,755	280	38	12	M(A)
Erato ...	...	...	...	...	1957	2,274	306	41	12	M(A)
Euterpe	...	...	...	...	1956	1,679	254	38	12	M(A)
Julin ...	...	...	...	...	1952	854	203	31	—	M(A)
Korbach	...	...	...	...	1955	1,710	247	39	12	M(A)
Urania	...	...	...	...	1956	1,421	244	38	—	M(A)

LENOX GES. FUR SCHIFFAHFT, G.m.b.H.

HAMBURG

FUNNEL: *Black with green device on white disc interrupting broad red band between two narrow green and white bands.*

HOUSEFLAG: *Red with white-edged green St. Andrew's cross and with a white disc containing a green device superimposed on the centre.*

Herford ...	...	...	...	1957	1,709	260	41	13	M(A)
I. G. Nichelson	...	...	...	1959	1,447	304	42	12½	M(A)
Vormann Rass	...	...	...	1956	999	220	33	11	M(A)

MATHIES REEDEREI K.G.

HAMBURG

FUNNEL: *Black with black letter "M" on white diamond on broad red band.*

HOUSEFLAG: *Red with black letter "M" on white diamond.*

Dalsland	...	...	...	...	1958	495	206	32	10½	M(A)
Gotaland	...	...	...	...	1957	493	206	32	10½	M(A)
Norrland	...	...	...	...	1951	2,170	285	12	12	M
Svealand	...	...	...	...	1950	2,170	285	41	12	M
Uppland	...	...	...	...	1955	293	184	30	10½	M(A)
Varmland	...	...	...	...	1950	299	154	26	10½	M(A)

OTTO A. MULLER

HAMBURG

FUNNEL: *Black with black device on white disc interrupting green over white over red bands.*

HOUSEFLAG: *Overall white diamond containing the black letters "O A M", the top triangular corners being green, the lower corners red.*

Birgit Muller	...	...	...	1957	499	181	29	—	M(A)
Else Muller ...	...	...	...	1952	996	216	35	12	M(A)
Gretchen Muller	...	...	...	1951	997	216	35	12	M(A)
Rethi Muller...	...	...	...	1961	999	234	36	12	M(A)

EGON OLDENDORFF

LUBECK

FUNNEL: *Black with white letters "E O" on broad blue band.*

HOUSEFLAG: *Blue with white letters "E O".*

Anna Oldendorff ...	...	...	1957	1,995	295	43	—	M(A)
Christiane Oldendorff	...	...	1962	2,980	347	50	—	M(2A)
Erna Oldendorff ...	...	...	1962	2,983	347	50	9	M(A)
Gebe Oldendorff ...	...	...	1940	1,528	255	38	9½	RT(A)
Gretke Oldendorff...	...	...	1921	1,319	247	37	9	SR
Hans Oldendorff ...	...	...	1962	2,983	347	50	9	M(2A)
Hille Oldendorff ...	...	...	1956	1,994	295	43	13	M(A)
Ilsabe Oldendorff ...	...	...	1951	2,619	203	44	—	SR
Imme Oldendorff ...	...	...	1953	1,670	274	41	12½	M(A)
Jobst Oldendorff ...	...	...	1928	2,388	349	49	13½	SR
Ludolf Oldendorff ...	...	...	1952	2,388	349	49	13½	M
Tete Oldendorff ...	...	...	1918	975	223	34	9	SR

Also larger Ocean Freighters.

H. PETERS REEDEREI

HAMBURG

FUNNEL: *Black with white letters "H P" on broad band between two narrow white bands.*

HOUSEFLAG: *Blue with deep white border at top and bottom and white letters "H P"*

Frieda Peters	...	...	...	1922	997	233	34	9	M
Hildegard Peters	...	...	...	1926	1,848	272	41	10	SR
Hinrich Peters	...	...	...	1952	2,611	310	46	—	M(A)
Margarete Peters	...	...	...	1953	958	207	33	—	M
Marthe Peters	...	...	...	1956	1,600	255	39	—	M(A)

M.V. Zaanstroom. Hollandsche S.M.   [*John G. Callis*

M.V. Admiralengracht. Spliethoffs Bevracht.   [*John G. Callis*

RENCK & HESSENMULLER

HAMBURG

FUNNEL: (*See introductory note*).

HOUSEFLAG:

All single-screw motorships with engines aft.

Anke Paul	...	...	341	Hammaburg	...	423	Mari	...	...	... 1,177
Bari	...	...	1,177	Hansa ...	...	299				
Bergland	...	...	341	Hove ...	...	497				

ERNST RUSS REEDEREI

HAMBURG

FUNNEL: *Black with red letters "E R" and red five-pointed star on broad white band.*

HOUSEFLAG: *White with red letters "E R" and red five-pointed star.*

Bottila Russ	...	...	...	...	1954	962	251	38	12	M(A)
Gisela Russ	...	...	...	...	1953	1,329	296	40	—	M(A)
Martha Russ	...	...	...	...	1949	1,478	296	43	11½	RT
Maria Russ	...	...	...	...	1960	1,412	306	41	—	M(A)
Reinhart-Lorenz Russ	...	...	...	1951	2,697	348	53	13	M
Tilly Russ	...	...	...	...	1949	1,485	296	43	11½	SR
Wolfgang Russ	...	...	...	...	1955	2,963	383	54	14½	M

SCHEPER'S RHEIN-SEE LINIE

HAMBURG

FUNNEL: *Yellow with narrow black top and broad blue band bearing red and white diagonally quartered houseflag.*

HOUSEFLAG: *Quartered diagonally red above and below white.*

Anna-Luise	...	...	300	Lippe ...	...	...	300	Rhein	...	... 299
Dinnislaken	...	...	425	Main ...	...	...	423	Saar	...	... 500
Ems	...	...	424	Mosel ...	...	...	299	Spree	...	... 425
Lahn	...	...	338	Neckar	...	...	380			

BERNARD SCHULTE A.G.

HAMBURG

FUNNEL: *Black with white letter "S" in red disc on broad green band.*

HOUSEFLAG: *Green with white letter "S" in red disc.*

Angelica Schulte	...	...	...	1958	1,307	256	41	13	M(A)
Christiane Schulte	...	...	1959	2,197	276	41	12½	M(A)
Elisabeth Henriette Schulte	...	1961	1,925	308	46	—	M(A)
Esther Charlotte Schulte	...	1961	1,918	308	46	—	M(A)

BERNARD SCHULTE A.G. (continued)

Heinrich Udo Schulte	...	...	1958	1,998	258	41	13	M(A)
Jan Ten Doornkaat	...	...	1961	1,918	310	46	—	M(A)
Johann Christian Schulte		...	1961	1,916	309	46	—	M(A)
Thomas Schulte	...	...	...	1957	1,319	256	41	13	M(A)
Wilhelm Schulte	...	...	...	1951	2,071	294	44	—	SR

SCHULTE & BRUNS

EMDEN

FUNNEL: *Black with white letters "S & B" superimposed on green over red bands.*

HOUSEFLAG: *Divided horizontally green over red, with white letters "S & B"*

Elisabeth Schulte	...	...	...	1956	2,285	284	42	—	M(A)
Elise Schulte	...	...	...	1958	1,879	259	39	—	M(2A)
Erika Schulte	...	...	...	1954	1,262	237	42	12½	M(A)
Erne Schulte	...	...	...	1965	—	—	—	—	M(A)
Gunther Schulte	...	...	...	1953	1,813	255	41	—	M(A)
Hermann Schulte	...	...	...	1953	1,967	258	41	12½	M(A)
Joachim Schulte	...	...	...	1950	2,734	316	43	—	M(2)
Lucie Schulte	...	...	...	1953	1,653	259	38	11½	M(A)
Maria Anna Schulte		...	...	1957	1,870	259	34	—	M(2A)

And larger ocean freighters.

ROBERT M. SLOMAN, Jr.

HAMBURG

FUNNEL: *Black with broad light green band.*

HOUSEFLAG: *Blue with white five-pointed star in each corner and white ship and castle device in centre.*

Alsterblick	...	...	...	...	1959	2,851	423	52	18½	M(A)
Alstertor	...	...	...	...	1952	2,460	391	47	16½	M
Alsterufer	...	...	...	...	1954	2,683	393	49	17	M
Lugano	...	...	...	...	1953	2,199	331	48	13¾	M
Sloman Algier	...	...	...	1951	1,376	284	42	13½	M
Sloman Malaga	...	...	...	1953	960	258	38	11½	M(A)
Sloman Messina	...	...	...	1951	1,377	284	42	13½	M
Sloman Palermo	...	...	...	1951	1,362	284	42	13½	M
Sloman Valencia	...	...	...	1951	1,362	284	42	13½	M
Tunis	...	...	...	...	1962	3,283	414	53	—	M

M.V. Timca. Spliethoff's Bevracht.   [*Fotoship*

M.V. Sonja D. Wagenborg.   [*Fotoship*

STERN LINIE
HEMMERSAM & HORNEMANN
LUBECK

FUNNEL: *Yellow with eight-pointed white star on green disc.*

HOUSEFLAG: *White with eight-pointed white star on green disc.*

Gemma	...	...	...	...	1952	320	170	27	—	M(A)
Maja ...	...	...	...	...	1957	1,056	261	41	—	M(A)
St. Patrick	...	...	...	...	1952	439	170	26	—	M(A)
Spika ...	...	...	...	...	1951	499	184	30	—	M(A)
Stella ...	...	...	...	...	1955	1,706	251	41	—	M(A)

JOHS. THODE
HAMBURG

FUNNEL: *Black with red letter "T" on white diamond on broad blue band.*

HOUSEFLAG:

Amazon II ...	...	350	Freiherr van Stein	299	Jurgen 293
Annaliese Wehlen ...		234	Geversdorf	384	Kondor 278
Annemarie ...	...	289	Gretel Maria... ...	221	Martin Lutje ... 499
Arn X ...	...	499	Gisela Happke ...	498	Nanna 298
Aventura ...	...	200	Gunther	349	Orion 239
Bokelnburg ...	...	498	Hamburg	388	Orion II 499
Charlotte ...	...	417	Hasselwerder ...	423	Rheinhard Danz ... 500
Claus Schriewer	...	299	Heimatland	424	Rugen 370
Dorothea Webber		387	Heinrich Knuppel ...	421	Seefalke 299
Duneck ...	...	424	Heinz Helmut ...	298	Traute 299
Drochtersen	...	388	Heinz Schriewer ...	246	Wallo 266
Emanuel II ...	...	495	Imperator	299	Welle 294
Erna Mayer ...	...	208	Inge Fielder	385	Wilhelm 424
Fortuna ...	...	270			

Iceland

ISLANDS H/F EIMSKIPAFELAG
ICELAND S.S. CO.
REYKJAVIK

FUNNEL: *White with narrow black top and separate broad blue band.*

HOUSEFLAG: *White with blue swastika device.*

SERVICES: *Reykjavik to Hull (Passenger and Cargo). Also services to North European ports from Copenhagen to Antwerp.*

Bakkafoss	...	...	...	...	1958	1,599	258	38	—	M(A)
Bruarfoss	...	...	...	...	1960	2,337	336	52	—	M
Dettifoss	...	...	...	...	1949	2,918	311	46	14	M
Fjallfoss	...	...	...	...	1954	1,796	305	43	13½	M(A)
Godafoss	...	...	...	...	1948	2,905	311	46	14	M
Gullfoss	...	...	...	...	1950	3,858	355	48	15½	M

Lagarfoss	...	...	...	...	1949	2,923	311	46	17	M
Manafoss	...	...	...	...	1959	498	217	32	—	M(A)
Reyjafoss	...	...	...	...	1947	2,553	295	42	11½	M
Selfoss...	...	...	...	...	1958	2,339	335	50	11	M(A)
Skogafoss	...	...	...	...	1965	1,837	314	45	—	M(A)
Tungufoss	...	...	...	...	1953	1,176	262	38	12¼	M(A)

Netherlands
BECK'S SCHEEPVAARTKANTOOR N.V.
ROTTERDAM

FUNNEL: *Bright blue with small red letter "B". (See introductory note).*

HOUSEFLAG:

Aiglon	...	...	336	Liberty	...	...	399	Valiant	...	...	499
Alert ...	...	...	395	Luctor	...	...	200	Vanda	...	...	400
Alpha	...	...	380	Neptunus	...	...	380	Velox ...	...	...	499
Cadans	...	...	499	Noblesse	...	...	397	Veritas	...	...	364
Comptesse	...	...	500	Proton	...	...	399	Vesta	...	...	500
Forel ...	...	...	350	Tarzan...	...	...	315	Victory	...	...	499
Gruno	...	...	400	Triton	...	...	400	Victress	...	...	399
Globe	...	...	367	Triumph	...	...	389	Viscount	...	...	388
Hunter	...	...	197	Tycha ...	...	...	499				

N.V. "CAREBEKA"
ROTTERDAM

FUNNEL: *Various. (See introductory note).*

All single-screw motorships with engines aft, except those marked * which have twin-screws.

Alcyone	...	...	364	Harm ...	...	...	492	Regina	...	...	313
Ali S ...	...	...	364	Helios	...	...	499	Repeto...	...	...	497
Alcor W	...	...	188	Hoop ...	...	...	499	Rifo-An	...	...	500
Aldebaran	...	...	399	Jan ...	...	...	500	Rubato	...	...	489
Alletta	...	...	469	Jannie ...	...	...	499	Rubicon	...	...	500
Ambulant	...	...	474	Jell ...	...	...	390	Salvinia	...	...	499
Argus	...	...	191	Karel ...	...	...	499	Setas ...	...	...	399
Arran*	...	...	500	Labrador	...	...	500	Sparta	...	...	399
Auriga G	...	...	398	Lifana	...	...	500	Speranza	...	...	383
Banka ...	...	...	499	Lauwers	...	...	499	Spes Major	...	...	499
Bianca	...	...	400	Ludo ...	...	...	500	Surte ...	...	...	244
Carebeka	...	...	500	Maas ...	...	...	299	Tasmanie	...	...	490
Carebeka II ...	...	499	Manta ...	...	...	366	Thea ...	...	...	500
Carebeka III	...	500	Maria W	...	...	299	Tiny ...	...	...	496
Cateli ...	...	...	399	Martini	...	...	400	Trianca	...	...	496
Citadel	...	...	369	Martje	...	...	399	Trinitas	...	...	499
Corona	...	...	386	Mees Cremer	...	395	Terschelling	...	500
Cresta	...	...	500	Merak ...	...	...	498	Tugro ...	...	...	400
Dievertje	...	...	499	Mount Everest	...	499	Union ...	...	...	315
Eddystone	...	...	475	Munte	...	...	496	Veendam	...	...	400
Emmy S	...	...	500	Nederland	...	...	335	Volente	...	...	257
Erebus	...	...	477	Nimrod	...	...	399	Volharding	...	...	488
Fivel ...	...	...	498	Noordzee	...	...	326	Voorwaarts	...	...	500
Flevo ...	...	...	499	Patria	...	...	341	Wegro	...	...	485
Fokke de Jong Sr.	...	400	Plancius	...	...	498	Wijmers	...	...	496
Gassolte	...	...	249	Polaris	...	...	353	Zwerver	...	...	196
Gersom	...	...	400	Prinses Wilhelmina		500				

M.V. Amstelborg. Wagenborg.

[D. R. Chesterton

M.V. Kroonborg. Wagenborg.

[D. Lynch

DAMMERS & VAN DER HEIDE'S SHIPPING & TRADING CO.

ROTTERDAM

FUNNEL: *White with narrow black top and blue band with red letter "D" thereon.*

HOUSEFLAG: *Blue with large red letter "D".*

All single-screw motorships with engines aft.

Anna Isabel ...	...	500	Francina	...	...	500	Risa Paula	...	...	1,426
Atlantic Star		...	499	Inca	...	...	1,427	Santa Maria	...	500
Biscaya	...	...	499	Johanna	...	499	Spolanda	...	499
Bonafide	...	...	500	Kenitra	...	499	Spolesto	...	...	500
Candide	...	...	500	Laura Christina	...	1,300	Sporonia	...	...	500
Casablanca	...	...	499	Malta	...	...	399	Tom van der Heide	500
Elisa ...	...	...	500	Matilda	...	...	499	Westzaan	...	...	500
Fedala	...	...	494	Maya ...	...	...	1,291		

GRONINGEN N.V. SCHEEPVAARTKANTOOR

GRONINGEN

FUNNEL: *Various. (See introductory note).*

All single-screw motorships with engines aft.

Arctic	...	...	500	Europa	...	...	257	Oceaan	...	...	498
Atlantic	...	...	498	Gitana	...	...	500	Pacific ...	...	...	499
Atlantide	...	...	500	Groningen	...	...	500	Paris ...	...	...	380
Brinda...	...	...	500	Harry ...	...	...	420	Tempo...	...	...	499
David	...	...	499	Jozina ...	...	...	500	Walcheren	...	...	400

"GRUNO" N.V. SCHEEPVAARTKANTOOR

AMSTERDAM

FUNNEL: *Yellow with blue band. (See introductory note).*

HOUSEFLAG:

All single-screw motorships with engines aft.

Afiena	...	...	400	Helena	...	...	500	Noordvaarder	...	499
Alge ...	...	...	350	Ida Jacobs	...	498	Noordstad	...	...	400
Alme	...	...	299	Irene ...	...	...	357	Patricia	...	...	400
Avenir	...	...	399	Irene-S	...	...	499	Port Talbot	...	250
Biak ...	...	...	499	Inspecteur Mellema	495	Raket ...	...	...	328
Biesbosch	...	...	329	Jonet ...	...	...	196	Skum ...	...	...	324
Bonanza	...	...	400	Kate ...	...	...	400	Sont ...	...	...	200
Cascade	...	...	341	Kazan ...	...	...	393	Spurt ...	...	...	500
Cawi ...	...	...	399	Lien ...	...	...	386	Speed ...	...	...	497
Ceta ...	...	...	400	Marathon	...	...	398	Start ...	...	...	203
Cito ...	...	...	359	Martha	...	...	500	Tasman	...	...	249
Cumulus	...	...	500	Marva ...	...	...	489	Tjoba ...	...	...	200
Diet ...	...	...	397	Marwit	...	...	499	Unitas	...	...	346
Emerald Isle	...	399	Martinistad	...	500	Vivat ...	...	...	438
Falcon	...	...	353	Menje ...	...	...	300	Wexford	...	...	200
Fambo	...	...	436	Merwestad	...	351	Wilja ...	...	...	289
Fendo ...	...	...	230	Metropole	...	...	294	Willemijn	...	...	478
Greta ...	...	...	377	Nelly	...	...	477	Wodan	...	...	400
Gronitas	...	...	279	Nolloth	...	...	347		

M. HAVINGA SCHEEPVAART & HANDELMAATS

GRONINGEN

FUNNEL: *Various. (See introductory note).*

HOUSEFLAG:

All single-screw motorships with engines aft.

Antilla	...	...	500	Duurt II	...	...	500	Result	...	...	...	457
Aruba	...	...	445	Hendrika Maria	...	499	Sylvia	...	...	...	500
Coeta	...	...	500	Jato	...	...	472	Sylvia II	...	...	500
Duurt	...	...	500	Marie Sophie	...	399	Willy	...	...	...	499

J. B. HOEKSTRA SCHEEP. N.V.

ROTTERDAM

FUNNEL: *Various. (See introductory note).*

HOUSEFLAG:

All single-screw motorships with engines aft.

Francisca	...	...	499	Ipswich Progress	...	333	Ipswich Purpose	...	333
Ipswich Pioneer	...	333							

A. C. HOFF

ROTTERDAM

FUNNEL: *Usually that of chartering company.*

HOUSEFLAG:

All single-screw motorships with engines aft.

Clipper	...	...	500	Goodwill Merchant	499	Goodwill Trader	...	500
Goodwill	...	...	500					

HOLLANDSCHE STOOMBOOT MAATS. N.V.

AMSTERDAM

FUNNEL: *Yellow with black top*

HOUSEFLAG: *White with red letters "H S M" and with small Netherlands ensign in top of hoist.*

SERVICES: *Amsterdam to Belfast, Bristol, Cardiff, Cork, Dublin, Fowey, Grangemouth, Hull, Leith, London, Manchester, Newport, Plymouth, Portsmouth, Shoreham, Swansea, Teignmouth and Waterford. Flushing to Shoreham (Cargo).*

Amstelstroom	...	...	...	1950	497	219	31	12½	M(A)
Berkelstroom	...	...	...	1962	489	195	30	12½	M(A)
Grebbestroom	...	...	...	1946	748	234	35	12	M(A)
Hontestroom	...	...	...	1957	500	225	33	12½	M(A)

M.V. Admiral Nelson. G. de Ruiter. [*Fotoship*

M.V. Maureen. Vereenigde Tankkustvaart N.V. Since Sold [*John G. Callis*

Ijstroom	...	...	...	...	1950	499	219	31	12½	M(A)
Texelstroom		...	...	...	1962	800	—	—	—	M(A)
Vechstroom	...	...	...	...	1952	496	225	31	12½	M(A)
Vliestroom	...	...	...	...	1957	500	189	30	—	M(A)
Zaanstroom	...	...	...	...	1952	496	225	31	12½	M(A)

Also larger Ocean Freighters.

C. HOLSCHERS KUSTVAARTBEDRIJF N.V.

FUNNEL: *Yellow with black letter "H" on white diamond on broad blue band.*
HOUSEFLAG: *Blue with black letter "H" on black-edged white diamond.*
All single-screw motorships with engines aft.

Arcturus	...	...	500	Hilda ...	...	...	250	Sonsbeek	...	...	427
Crescendo	...	...	348	Idanel	...	...	297	Taurus	...	...	310
Gloria Maris		...	1,426	Joma ...	...	...	496	Timo ...	...	...	199
Helen ...	...	...	199	Lydia ...	...	...	397	Vindicat	...	...	500
Hermes	...	...	500	Mercurius H.		...	457	Virgo	...	...	397
Helvetias	...	...	494							

HOLWERDA SCHEEPVAART N.V.

HEERENVEERN

FUNNEL:
HOUSEFLAG:
All single-screw motorships with engines aft.

Avanti...	...	...	448	Harlingen	...	...	500	Spray ...	...	...	239
Cornelius				Pollendam	...	...	500	Tjerk Hiddes		...	479
Van der Schoot	...	500	Roelof Holwerda	...	383	Zwartewater		...	336
Expansa	...	...	489							

HUDIG & VEDER N.V.

ZEEVAART N.V. MIJ

ROTTERDAM

FUNNEL: *Black with blue star on broad white band.*
HOUSEFLAG: *White with blue letters "H & V" and with blue star in top of hoist.*
PASSENGER AND CARGO SERVICE: *Rotterdam and Antwerp to Dublin and Belfast.*

Echo ...	...	...	...	...	1961	1,855	290	42	—	M(A)
Hagno...	...	...	...	...	1960	1,139	256	37	15	M(A)
Thallo	...	...	...	...	1951	499	229	32	13	M(A)
Theano	...	...	...	...	1952	1,020	257	39	13½	M(A)
Trito ...	...	...	...	...	1953	1,030	257	39	13½	M(A)

Also larger ocean freighters.

HUDIG & PIETERS' ALGEMEENE N.V.

ROTTERDAM

FUNNEL: *Yellow with black top.*

HOUSEFLAG: *Blue with white rectangle at centre and with red St. George's cross superimposed: the white letters "H & P" diagonally from top of hoist.*

All single-screw motorships with engines aft.

Export II	...	...	474	Jacaranda	...	...	499	Meidoorn	...	...	500

W. H. JAMES & CO. SHEEPV. & HANDEL MAATS. N.V.

ROTTERDAM

FUNNEL: *Yellow.*

HOUSEFLAG:

All single-screw motorships with engines aft.

Catharina	...	...	499	Lely	...	...	...	499	Senang	...	...	496
Frejo	...	...	500	Netta	...	...	...	499	Zeester	...	...	498
Leemans	...	...	496	Rose	...	...	...	496	Zus	...	...	493

KAMPMAN'S BEVRACHT EN CONTROLBEDRIJF

AMSTERDAM

FUNNEL: *Various. (See introductory note).*

All single-screw motorships with engines aft.

Arbon	...	...	500	Herman Buisman	...	400	Phoenix	...	...	500
Bern	...	...	500	Jans	...	...	...	388	Pirola...	...	...	488
Bresam	...	...	499	Margriet L	...	...	500	Roelof Buisman	...	400
Buka	...	...	198	Mutua Fides	...	...	302	Transit	...	...	499
Carasso	...	...	500	Nanning Buisman	...	491	Tubo	...	...	500
Energie	...	...	400	Nieuwe Waterweg		382	Waverstroom	...	489
Francois Buisman	...	497	Pandora	...	...	399	Westerdok	...	393
Geertje Buisman	...	1,174	Pegasus	...	...	399			

KAMP'S SCHEEPVAART EN HANDELMAATS N.V.

GRONINGEN

FUNNEL: *Yellow with broad white band. (See introductory note).*

HOUSEFLAG:

All single-screw motorships with engines aft.

Aaltje...	...	...	200	Baltic	...	...	397	Democrat	...	...	198
Adriana	...	...	198	Cheetah	...	...	499	Denzo	...	...	184
Agnes...	...	...	386	Curacao	...	...	334	Dita Smits	...	...	499
Anholt	...	...	262	Da Costa	...	...	400	Dita Smits II	...	...	454
Appingedam	...	500	Deborah	...	...	307	Eagle	...	...	386

Fen	...	...	200	Kirsten Smits	...	500	Olwe ...	...	...	399
Finlandia	...	...	381	Lloyd	...	498	Orient	...	...	499
Fivelstad	...	...	500	Louise Smits	...	499	Pial	...	...	307
Garonne	...	...	390	Lovesteyn	...	384	Quo Vadis	...	...	499
Gea-M	...	...	221	Madjoe	...	499	Sagitta	...	...	399
Gironde	...	...	400	Majorca	...	500	Texel	...	...	200
Hado	...	...	310	Margarita Smits	...	499	Vrede	...	...	398
Hasewint	...	...	499	Margriet Anja	...	498	Wega ...	...	...	346
Hoc Vinces	...	...	352	Marinus Smits	...	499	Westland Producer			366
Hollandia	...	...	327	Minerva II	...	480	Westland Trader	...		295
Jaguar	...	...	498	Nautic	...	495	Wim II	...	...	499
Janny ...	...	...	248	Navis	...	498	Zuiderzee	...	...	499
Johnny...	...	...	500	Neerlandia	...	400				
Kars	...	...	352	Nike	...	367				

LIBERG SCHEEPVAARTKANTOOR
RAAMSDOKSVEER

FUNNEL: *Black with broad white band.*

HOUSEFLAG:
All single-screw motorships with engines aft.

Cornelis Houtmann	499	Olivier van Noort...	496	Willem Barendsz ...	400
Keizersveerz	...	500				

MARITIMA SCHEEP. & HANDEL MAATS., N.V.
FUNNEL:

HOUSEFLAG:
All single-screw motorships with engines aft.

Aegir ...	...	...	195	Dolores	...	...	499	Meta ...	...	...	265
Amasus	...	...	230	Eemshorn	...	...	237	Meeuw	...	...	390
Baltic ...	...	...	397	Fluvius...	...	...	335	Njord ...	...	...	456
Bara ...	...	...	465	Forto ...	...	...	370	Rapid ...	...	...	296
Catharina W		...	224	Hebe Nobel ...	...	...	196	Reiger ...	...	...	200
Castor...	...	...	199	Kolga ...	...	...	399				
Diet ...	...	...	397	Lutetia	...	...	191				

Wm. H. MULLER & CO. N.V.
ROTTERDAM

FUNNEL: *Black with large white letter "M" on broad red band between two narrow white bands.*

HOUSEFLAG: *White with broad vertical red band bearing the white letters "Wm H M & Co" between two narrow white lines.*

CARGO SERVICES: *London to Antwerp–Rouen–Paris–Casablanca; Liverpool to Rouen and Paris; Manchester to Rouen and Paris; Glasgow to Rouen and Paris; King's Lynn to Rotterdam; Boston to Rotterdam; Middlesbrough to Amsterdam and Rotterdam; Aberdeen to Rotterdam; London to Rotterdam; Chatham to Rotterdam.*

Aardenburgh	...	...	...	1938	499	178	29	10	M(A)
Batavier I	...	...	...	1949	498	205	32	11	M(A)

Wm. H. MULLER & CO. N.V. (*continued*)

Batavier III	...	...	...	...	1949	498	205	32	11	M(A)
Batavier V	...	...	...	...	1958	499	249	34	13½	M(A)
Brittenburgh		...	...	...	1961	458	199	31	11	M(A)
Domburgh	...	...	...	...	1949	991	254	40	13½	M(A)
Nijenburgh	...	...	...	...	1939	400	155	26	9½	M(A)
Oosterburgh		...	...	...	1953	499	179	31	11	M(A)
Poolster	...	...	...	...	1962	1,070	300	40	—	M2(A)
Rozenburgh	...	...	...	...	1958	499	164	26	10	M(A)
Sandenburgh		...	...	...	1957	488	165	26	—	M(A)
Trompenburgh		...	...	...	1940	385	163	28	9½	M(A)
Vrijburgh	...	...	...	...	1949	991	264	40	13½	M(A)
Walenburgh	...	...	...	...	1938	496	176	29	11	M(A)
Zeeburgh	...	...	...	...	1964	499	236	34	13	M(A)

NIEUWE KUSTVAART MAATS.

AMSTERDAM

FUNNEL: *Black with two widely spaced white bands.*

HOUSEFLAG:

All single-screw motorships with engines aft.

Aeneas	...	...	496	Calchas	...	...	499	Mithras	...	...	499
Alcetas	...	...	496	Ilias	...	...	499	Mynias	...	...	499
Amyntas	...	...	499	Labotas	...	...	500	Pallas	...	...	499
Arcas	...	...	499	Leonidas	...	...	499	Phidias	...	...	496
Ardeas	...	...	496	Libertas	...	...	499	Philetas	...	...	496
Atlas	...	...	487	Magas	...	...	499	Targas	...	...	499
Boreas	...	...	499	Midas	...	...	488	Thaletas	...	...	499

Also larger Ocean Freighters.

J. J. ONNES

GRONINGEN

FUNNEL: *Yellow with broad blue band.*

HOUSEFLAG:

All single-screw motorships with engines aft.

Anja	...	...	...	262	Bram	...	...	...	398	Ritornel	...	...	199
Ardito	...	...	...	500	Jurgen de Vries	...	500	Wartiena	...	...	365

OOST ATLANTIQUE LIJN N.V.

OTTO BOSMA

ROTTERDAM

FUNNEL:

HOUSEFLAG:

All single-screw motorships with engines aft.

Arnhem	...	...	500	Cornelius B III	...	500	Spes	...	...	...	424
Cornelius B II	...	488	Cornelius B IV	...	499				

ROTTERDAMSCHE KUSTVAART CENTRALE N.V.
ROTTERDAM

FUNNEL: *Yellow with narrow black top and separate narrow blue band, below which a white letter "R" on a red disc is outlined in white and blue.*

HOUSEFLAG:

All single-screw motorships with engines aft.

Betty-Anne S	...	499	Gerry S	...	...	500	Pieter S	...	...	1,929

G. DE RUITER'S KUSTVAART REEDEREI
THE HAGUE

FUNNEL: *Yellow with houseflag on white diamond.*

HOUSEFLAG: *Red over white over blue pennant with black letters "GR" on white.*

All single-screw motorships with engines aft.

Admiral Courbet	...	489	Admiral Nelson	...	363	Myra	...	...	...	489

SCHEEPVAART-EN-STEENKOLEN MAATS. N.V.
ROTTERDAM

FUNNEL: *Black with blue diamond on broad white band between two narrow red bands.*

HOUSEFLAG: *Four blue bands interrupted with three red bands with a white diamond bearing the black letters "S S M" superimposed.*

CARGO SERVICES: *Dutch ports to Boston and King's Lynn. (In association with the British associated company, Shipping & Coal Co. London)*

Beijerland	...	...	...	...	1957	479	212	31	12	M(A)
Flevoland	...	...	...	...	1955	388	210	31	12½	M(A)
Friesland	...	...	...	...	1950	2,788	314	44	10½	M(A)
Gaasterland	...	...	...	...	1940	375	208	30	11	M(A)
Hoogland	...	...	...	...	1956	1,499	240	38	11½	M(A)
Nieuwland	...	...	...	...	1951	689	236	36	12	M
Sint Annaland	...	...	...	...	1960	500	225	33	12	M(A)
Sint Jansland	...	...	...	...	1962	500	225	33	—	M(A)
Sint Philipsland	...	...	...	...	1962	500	224	33	—	M(A)
Westland	...	...	...	...	1963	500	225	33	—	M(A)

SCHELLEN SCHEEPVAART N.V.
ROTTERDAM

FUNNEL: *Black with broad red band bearing a white "Swiss" cross.*

HOUSEFLAG:

All single-screw motorships with engines aft.

Adine	...	...	438	Juvelta	...	...	499	Silvretta	...	...	437
Bernina	...	...	428	Realta	...	...	433	Willem Cornelis	...		500
Casana	...	...	250	Silvaplana	...	...	442				

M.V. Heemraadssingel. P.A. Van Es & Co. [*John G. Callis*

M.V. Roelof Buisman. [*John. G. Callis*

SPLIETHOFF'S BEVRACHTTINGSKANTOOR N.V.

AMSTERDAM

FUNNEL: *Yellow with black "S" on four coloured panel as houseflag.*

HOUSEFLAG: *Quartered diagonally orange over red, blue over white with black letter "S" in centre.*

All single-screw motorships with engines aft.

Admiralengracht	...	500	Heerengracht	...	493	Prinsenbeek	...	500
Aerdenhout	...	500	Hoorneboeg ...	...	499	Prinsengracht	...	500
Berkhout	...	500	Housterhoot...	...	500	Schoonebeek	...	500
Bloemgracht	...	500	Keizersgracht	...	497	Timca	...	499
Eerbeck ...	...	499	Lauriergracht	...	500	Trica	...	498
Elshout ...	...	500	Leliegracht ...	...	499	Wedlooper ...	...	500
Genca	...	498						

P. A. VAN ES & CO. N.V.

ROTTERDAM

FUNNEL: *Black with white "V E" monogram in white edged red disc.*

HOUSEFLAG: *Three green and two white horizontal stripes with white diamond containing black V E monogram inside a black circle at centre.*

All single-screw motorships with engines aft except **Bernisse** which has engines amidship.

Bernisse ...	...	756	Diana ...	...	500	Lindesingel ...	...	500
Boezensingel	...	352	Erasmussingel	...	400	Meidoornsingel	...	500
Bree-Helle ...	...	499	Goote ...	...	490	Molensingel ...	...	500
Breezand ...	...	499	Hoyledesingel	...	400	Spoorsingel ...	...	500
Breehorn ...	...	499	Imber ...	...	496	Urkersingel ...	...	498
Breewiyd ...	...	494	Kerksingel ...	...	498	Vermeersingel	...	496
Carnissesingel	...	499	Kittiwake ...	...	496			

VEREENIGDE TANKKUSTVAART N.V.

Marcolla (Tkr)	...	575	Maud ...	...	...	...	499	Melissa	...	...	499

VAN GEEST, WALING & ZN.

AMSTERDAM

FUNNEL: *White with re-bordered yellow diamond containing a red letter "G" interrupting two narrow blue bands.*

HOUSEFLAG: *White with design as on funnel.*

Geestdam	...	...	...	...	1958	335	153	24	—	M(A)
Geestdiep	...	...	...	...	1961	360	162	25	—	M(A)
Geestdijk	...	...	...	...	1956	318	147	24	—	M(A)
Geestsluis	...	...	...	...	1962	359	—	—	—	M(A)
Geeststroom	...	...	...	1954	318	144	23	—	M(A)

Also larger ships.

VAN UDEN'S SCHEEPVAART N.V.

ROTTERDAM

FUNNEL: *Black with blue letter "U" in white diamond on broad blue band.*
HOUSEFLAG: *Blue with blue letter "U" on large white diamond.*
All single-screw motorships with engines aft.

Binnenhaven...	...	488	Merwehaven...	...	499	Schiehaven	...	...	499
Coccinelle	...	...	500	Nassauhaven...	...	397	Yselhaven	...	...	499
Leuvehaven	...	...	357						

Also larger Ocean Freighters.

VEREENIGDE CARGODOORSKANTOOR, N.V.

THE HAGUE

FUNNEL: *Black with green and yellow circular device.*
HOUSEFLAG:
All single-screw motorships with engines aft.

Ask	...	...	499	Embla ...	...	...	499	Normandia	...	...	432
Burgundia	...	...	432	Gefle	...	...	469	Rossen	...	...	381
Edda	...	...	500	Mangen	...	...	499	Unden	...	...	499
Elisabeth	...	...	489	Marianne	...	...	390	Vega	...	...	500
Ella	...	...	394	Nore	...	...	495	Vesta	...	...	420

J. VERMAS SCHEEPVAARTBEDRIJF

ROTTERDAM

FUNNEL: *Yellow with narrow black top and black letter "V" on white panel. (See introductory note).*
HOUSEFLAG: *Blue with white diagonal stripe containing the black letters "V.S.B".*

Atlantis	...	...	...	...	1958	500	193	29	10	M(A)
Barendsz	...	...	...	...	1954	500	180	30	10	M(A)
Erasmus	...	...	...	...	1952	1,324	235	35		M(A)
Evertsen	...	...	...	...	1962	499	184	30	10	M(A)
Heemskerk	...	...	...	1955	500	183	30	10	M(A)
Henny J	...	...	...	...	1949	410	156	25		M(A)
Houtman	...	...	...	...	1955	500	183	30	10	M(A)
Ingkabir	...	...	...	...	1964	499	185	30	10	M(A)
Jongkind	...	...	...	...	1953	499	184	30	10	M(A)
Keyser	...	...	...	...	1942	499	183	30	10	M(A)
Laga	...	...	...	...	1960	1,871	278	40	10	M(A)
Lies	...	...	...	...	1949	498	181	28	9	M(A)
Lubox	...	...	...	...	1957	500	184	30	10	M(A)
Mies	...	...	...	...	1951	500	190	29	9½	M(A)
Naerebout	...	...	...	1957	499	198	31	10	M(A)
Noord...	...	...	...	...	1956	500	193	30	10	M(A)
Prosperite	...	...	...	1956	500	183	30	10	M(A)
Robox	...	...	...	...	1956	499	189	29		M(A)
Skadi	...	...	...	...	1960	1,871	278	40	10	M(A)
Steven...	...	...	...	...	1957	1,993	258	41	12½	M(A)
Swindregt	...	...	...	1962	499	234	34	11	M(A)
Tromp	...	...	...	...	1958	500	184	30	10	M(A)
Van Brakel	...	...	...	1958	500	184	28	10	M(A)

Margaretha Smits. Kamo's Scheepvaart.   [*D. Lynch*

M.V. Dido. Chr. J. Reim.   [*John G. Callis*

M.V. Brielle. F. Olsen & Co.   [*D. R. Chesterton*

I   129

JOHN B. VETS & CO.

ANTWERP

FUNNEL: *Yellow with narrow black top.*

HOUSEFLAG:

All single-screw motorships with engines aft.

| Albert Willem | ... | 428 | Olive ... | ... | ... | 337 | Teun | ... | ... | ... | 468 |
| Isis | ... | ... | 468 | | | | | | | | |

Belgian-owned registered under the Netherlands flag.

WAGENBORG'S SCHEEPVAART N.V.

ROTTERDAM

FUNNEL: *Black with two white bands.* (*See introductory note*).

HOUSEFLAG: *Quartered diagonally red over white over red, with reproduction of funnel at centre.*

All single-screw motorships with engines aft.

Advent	...	333	Els Teekman	...	399	Nassauborg ...	...	499
Ahoy	...	369	Esperance	...	236	Niagara	...	500
Albatross	...	297	Favoriet	...	500	Noordborg	...	400
Alja V	...	200	Fem	...	399	Noorderkroon	...	500
Amstelborg	...	500	Fiona	...	400	Noordkaap	...	461
Antarctica	...	375	Fivelborg	...	281	Oosterdiep	...	387
Arneborg	...	332	Frisia	...	350	Oranjeborg	...	498
Balticborg	...	1,570	Geja	...	200	Paul Westers	...	473
Batavier	...	448	Goeree	...	204	Pavonis	...	384
Beppie	...	500	Gouweborg	...	394	Pergo ...	...	383
Berkelborg	...	397	Grada Westers	...	400	Prinsenborg	...	499
Bevesier	...	400	Gratia ...	...	289	Reestborg	...	400
Bothniaborg	...	1,577	Hendrik B	...	200	Reggeborg	...	299
Brinio	...	346	Herta	...	296	Rien Teekman	...	499
Calvijn	...	373	Horizon	...	200	Rijnborg	...	454
Caravelle	...	350	Hunzeborg	...	397	Roerdomp	...	350
Chrysant	...	248	Ida D	...	494	Scheldeborg	...	394
Clothilda M	...	342	Ijsselborg	...	376	Schieborg	...	397
Coenraad K	...	454	Jacob Teekman	...	396	Schokland	...	298
Delfborg	...	387	Jan Brins	...	467	Spaarneborg	...	392
Dicky ...	...	499	Jantje Eppiena	...	376	Steady	...	370
Dinah	...	388	Jenjo	...	200	Stella Maris	...	300
Dinkel	...	200	Kroonborg	...	499	Thalassa	...	499
Dintelborg	...	397	Lauwersborg	...	298	Trude-K	...	293
Dollard	...	496	Lingeborg	...	394	Uranus B	...	290
Donau	...	357	Lireco ...	...	349	Ursa Minor	...	386
Dongeburg	...	399	Louise ...	...	400	Vanessa	...	500
Draka ...	...	498	Luise Emilie	...	500	Vetchborg	...	399
Drenthe	...	469	Lydia W	...	387	Vera ...	...	332
Drie Gebroeders	...	500	Maasborg	...	473	Waalborg	...	499
Dubhe	...	499	Makkum	...	335	Westereems	...	500
Edison	...	498	Marconi	...	499	Zaanborg	...	392
Eems ...	...	477	Markborg	...	499	Zanzibar	...	387
Eemsborg	...	499	Martenshoek...	...	478	Zeevaart	...	359
Eemsmond	...	456	Merweborg	...	500	Zwaartiena	...	385
Egbert Wagenborg		498						

N. V. STOOM MAATS. WESTPOLDER
AMSTERDAM

FUNNEL: *Yellow with black top and black letter "W" on white diamond on broad green band.*

HOUSEFLAG: *Green with black letter "W" on large white diamond.*

CARGO SERVICES: *Amsterdam to Chatham and the Thames.*

All single-screw motorships with engines aft.

Arnoudspolder	...	442	Emmapolder	...	500	Oranjepolder	...	500

WIJNNE & BARENDS N.V.
GRONINGEN

FUNNEL: *Yellow. (See introductory note).*

HOUSEFLAG:

All single-screw motorships with engines aft.

Adara	...	...	324	Golina	...	...	384	Noorster	...	...	285
Alberta	...	...	314	Gre	...	...	200	Nora	...	...	467
Alderd-L	...	...	384	Henny T	...	...	494	Nova Zembla	...	200
Ali	...	...	388	Hinde	...	...	400	Olympia	...	...	500
Amazone	...	...	500	Hondsbosch	...	...	217	Oranje	...	...	231
Annie G	...	...	249	Jean E	...	...	455	Paloma	...	...	493
Arizona	...	...	500	Johanca	...	...	500	Pamir	...	...	300
Audrey Johanna	...	442	Johanna	...	...	238	Riet	...	...	427
Beta	...	...	399	Johannes	...	...	493	Rini	...	...	298
Bonaire	...	...	400	Juno	...	...	400	Roelof Jan	...	500
Borelly	...	...	430	Jupiter	...	...	500	Saba	...	...	400
Canada	...	...	451	Jutland	...	...	500	Santa Lucia	...	396
Capella	...	...	498	Kon-Tiki	...	...	385	Santa Margherita	...	500
Carmen	...	...	451	Lea	...	...	359	Senior	...	...	374
Catherina-F	...	338	Lenie	...	...	400	Solent	...	...	297
Celebes	...	...	498	Lizard	...	...	300	Spica	...	...	494
Confid	...	...	200	Lucy	...	...	450	Tagri	...	...	274
Corsica	...	...	242	Lumie	...	...	415	Telstar	...	...	500
Deo Duce	...	...	500	Marie	...	...	494	Tide	...	...	399
Deo Gloria	...	...	500	Marie Christine	...	390	Tinda	...	...	453
Deo Gratias	...	...	399	Mars	...	...	200	Viola	...	...	398
Diannel	...	...	397	Mascotte	...	...	399	Willem Fortuin	...	341
Donata	...	...	200	Mathilde	...	...	448	Wuta	...	...	158
Equator	...	...	493	Menna	...	...	470	Ysel	...	...	297
Frans W	...	...	396	Meteoor	...	...	500	Zephyr	...	...	500
Geert	...	...	353	Nomadisch	...	...	363	Zuidpool	...	...	491
Glory	...	...	323	Noorderhaven	...	376	Zwaluw	...	...	200

ZEELAND SHIPPING CO. LTD.
FLUSHING

FUNNEL: *Yellow with black top separated by red over white over blue bands.*

HOUSEFLAG: *Blue with white St. Andrew's Cross with crown superimposed at centre.*

PASSENGER SERVICE: *Hook of Holland–Harwich. (Day service in conjunction with British Rail's night service over the same route).*

Koningen Emma	...	...	...	1939	4,253	380	47	23	M(2)
Koningen Wilhelmina	...	...	1960	6,228	393	57	24	M(2)
Prinses Beatrix	...	...	...	1939	4,353	380	47	23	M(2)

ZUID HOLLANDSCHE SCHEEPVAART MAATS., N.V.

AMSTERDAM

FUNNEL: *Black with diagonal white band on green panel.*

HOUSEFLAG: *Green with diagonal white band.*

All single-screw motorships with engines aft.

Driebergen ...	...	495	Maarsbergen	...	499	Ubbergen ...	...	499
Gramsbergen	...	498	Rijsbergen ...	...	498	Zevenbergen...	...	498
Huybergen ...	...	499	Steenbergen ...	...	499			

Norway

BERGENSKE DAMPSKIBSSELSKAB
BERGEN LINE

BERGEN

FUNNEL: *Black, or yellow, with three white rings.*

HOUSEFLAG: *Red swallowtail with blue and white border at top and bottom and the white letters "B D S" over a white star in centre.*

SERVICES: *Stavanger and Bergen–Newcastle (Passenger). West Norwegian ports to Newcastle, Liverpool and Manchester, and London (Cargo). Cruises from Newcastle or Dover to Norway, etc., and from Southampton or Plymouth to Madeira. Also services from Norway to European ports and to South America.*

Canopus	...	...	...	...	1948	1,335	264	40	12	M
Corvus	...	...	...	...	1947	1,333	264	40	12	M
Leda ...	...	...	...	...	1952	6,670	410	57	22	ST(2)
Mercur	...	...	...	...	1946	939	235	35	12½	M
Meteor	...	...	...	...	1954	2,856	297	45	18	M
Venus ...	...	...	...	...	1931	6,269	421	54	20	M(2)

Other ships are: **Ara, Astraea, Capella, Carina, Cygnus, Delfinus, Deneb, Diana, Draco, Estrella, Iris, Leo, Luna, Lynx, Midnatsol, Nordlys, Nordstjernen, Pallas, Polarlys, Sirius, Uranus, Ursa, Vela.** Also larger ocean ships.

FEARNLEY & EGER
A/S STANDARD

OSLO

FUNNEL: *Black with blue Maltese cross on white panel on broad red band.*

HOUSEFLAG: *Red with blue Maltese cross on large white panel.*

Stalheim	...	...	...	...	1959	1,521	289	41	12	M(A)
Stanford	...	...	...	...	1959	1,523	289	41	12	M(A)

Also larger ocean freighters.

D/S HAFNIA A/S.
ODENSE

FUNNEL: *Blue with black top and white letters "T C".*

HOUSEFLAG:

Fursund	...	...	...	...	1956	1,082	224	35	—	M(A)
Vilsund	...	...	...	...	1961	1,234	242	36	—	M(A)

Also the smaller **Alssund** and **Brosund.**

FRIDTJOF KRISTIANSEN
OSLO

FUNNEL: *Yellow with black top and white letters "F K" on green panel.*

HOUSEFLAG: *Green with white letters "F K".*

Ingrid K	...	...	...	...	1962	497	227	33	—	M(A)
Ragnhild K	...	...	...	...	1956	498	217	33	—	M(A)
Sigrid K	...	...	...	...	1961	500	227	33	—	M(A)

EGIL NAESHEIM A/S.
HAUGESAND

FUNNEL: *Yellow with narrow black top and white "E N" monogram on broad red band.*

HOUSEFLAG: *Red with white "E N" monogram.*

Vard	...	...	...	...	...	1930	1,938	283	43	10	SR
Vardal ..	...	...	...	...	1921	1,546	263	38	9½	SR
Varodd	...	...	...	...	1958	1,921	269	40	10	·M(A)

DET NORDENFJELSKE D/S A/S.
TRONDHEIM

FUNNEL: *Black with broad red band between two narrow white bands.*

HOUSEFLAG: *White with red rose device surrounded by coiled rope in centre and the black letters "N F D S" in each corner.*

SERVICES: *Grimsby to Stavanger and Norwegian coastal ports. Also Norwegian coastal services.*

Atle Jarl	...	...	...	...	1947	1,333	264	40	12	M
Erik Jarl	...	...	...	...	1955	454	184	29	11	M
Erling Jarl	...	...	...	...	1949	2,125	269	41	15	M
Eystein Jarl ...	...	...	...	1949	1,013	236	35	12	M
Guttorm Jarl	...	...	...	1947	935	202	33	11½	M(A)
Hakon Jarl ...	...	...	...	1952	2,173	265	40	15	M(2)
Harald Jarl ...	...	...	...	1960	2,568	287	44	16	M(A)
Knut Jarl	...	...	...	...	1949	1,026	236	35	12	M
Ragnvald Jarl	...	...	...	1956	2,196	268	41	16	M(A)
Sigurd Jarl ...	...	...	...	1962	1,380	239	38	—	M(A)

Sote Jarl	...	...	...	...	1962	1,389	239	38	—	M(A)
Tore Jarl	...	...	...	...	1956	839	227	36	12½	M(A)
Torfinn Jarl		...	...	...	1956	839	226	36	12	M(A)

Also larger Ocean Freighters.

FRED SOLEN & CO.
OSLO

FUNNEL: *Yellow, or black, with replica of houseflag.*

HOUSEFLAG: *White swallow tail with diagonal blue stripe from top of hoist and blue disc on top of fly.*

SERVICES: *Oslo and Kristiansund to Newcastle (Passenger). Norwegian ports to Grangemouth, Middlesbrough and London (Cargo). Also services from Norwegian ports, London, Southampton and Dieppe to Spain, Portugal and Mediterranean and Canary Isles.*

Baalbek	...	...	...	...	1937	2,164	330	44	13	M
Baden ...	...	...	...	...	1937	1,400	273	39	13½	SR
Baldrian	...	...	...	...	1947	1,316	277	42	11	M
Balduin	...	...	...	...	1955	2,224	290	43	13½	M
Bamse	...	...	...	...	1947	1,701	272	42	10½	SR
Banaderos	...	...	...	...	1953	2,269	342	47	—	M
Bajamar	...	...	...	...	1953	2,272	342	47	—	M
Barlind	...	...	...	...	1939	1,524	274	41	11	M
Barok	...	...	...	...	1950	1,140	257	38	12	M(A)
Basel ...	...	...	...	...	1962	298	178	29	—	M(A)
Bengazi	...	...	...	...	1947	2,173	350	47	—	M
Binna	...	...	...	...	1952	1,858	284	44	11½	SR(2)
Biri ...	...	...	...	...	1957	499	216	33	12	M(A)
Blenheim	...	...	...	...	1951	4,766	374	53	16	M
Bolt	...	...	...	...	1950	1,030	258	38	12	M(A)
Bolzano	...	...	...	...	1949	1,689	302	43	13	M(A)
Bomma	...	...	...	...	1949	1,029	258	38	12½	M(A)
Bonn ...	...	...	...	...	1962	298	178	30	12¾	M(A)
Borre	...	...	...	...	1949	1,029	258	38	12½	M(A)
Brabant	...	...	...	...	1956	2,194	290	42	13	M(A)
Braemar	...	...	...	...	1952	4,776	374	53	—	M
Bravo	...	...	...	...	1943	1,864	312	42	12	M
Breda	...	...	...	...	1957	1,462	291	42	—	M(A)
Brielle...	...	...	...	...	1962	298	174	29	—	M(A)
Bruin ...	...	...	...	...	1955	1,879	285	44	8½	SR
Brunla...	...	...	...	...	1961	499	203	36	—	M(A)
Bruse ...	...	...	...	...	1961	499	244	35	—	M(A)
Bysanz	...	...	...	...	1947	2,126	335	45	—	M

Also larger ocean ships.

CHR. J. REIM
A/S DIONE
PORSGRUNN

FUNNEL: *Black with green band between two white bands.*

HOUSEFLAG: *Green with green letter "R" in white diamond.*

Diala	...	...	...	...	1952	1,742	258	38	11	M(A)
Dido ...	...	...	...	...	1949	1,617	258	38	11	M(A)
Dione	...	...	...	...	1956	2,668	259	44	10½	M(2A)
Disa ...	...	...	...	...	1959	2,864	297	44	—	M(A)
Divina	...	...	...	...	1950	1,699	258	38	11	M(A)
Dixie ...	...	...	...	...	1946	1,578	255	38	11	MT(A)

KJELL RINDE

OSLO

FUNNEL: *Yellow with narrow black top and separate narrow blue band with, below, a white letter "R" on a red disc outlined in white and blue.*

HOUSEFLAG: *Blue with white letter "R" on white disc outlined in white.*

Peter Rinde	...	...	...	1957	1,885	274	40	12½	M(A)
Sigurd Rinde	...	...	...	1957	1,885	274	40	12½	M(A)

OTTO THORESEN SHIPPING CO.

OSLO

FUNNEL:

HOUSEFLAG:

SERVICES: *Southampton to Cherbourg and Le Havre (Passenger and Car Ferry).*

Viking I	...	...	...	...	1964	3,608	326	60	—	M(2)
Viking II	...	...	...	...	1964	3,611	326	60	—	M(2)
Viking III	...	...	...	...	1965	3,600	326	60	—	M(2)

Poland

POLSKIE LINIE OCEANICZNE P.P.

POLISH OCEAN LINES

GDYNIA

FUNNEL: *White with red and white shield with the arms of Poland interrupting red band between two narrow white bands.*

HOUSEFLAG: *White, with shield as on funnel interrupting single horizontal red stripe.*

SERVICES: *Gdynia and Gdansk to London and Hull (Passenger). Also other world-wide passenger and cargo routes from Polish ports.*

Deblin	...	...	...	...	1961	1,265	268	40	15	M
Koszalin	...	...	...	...	1960	1,273	268	40	15	SR
Jaroslwa Dabrowski		...	...	1950	3,196	337	48	13	M
Wolin	...	...	...	...	1959	1,272	268	40	15	M

M.V. Viking III. Otto Thoresen Shpg Ltd. *[John G. Callis*

M.V. Loke. Stokholms Red "Svea". *[John G. Callis*

M.V. Magne. Stockholms Red "Svea". *[D. R. Chesterton*

POLSKA ZEGLUGA MORSKA
POLISH STEAMSHIP CO.
GDYNIA

FUNNEL: *Black with red and white shield with arms of Poland interrupting red band between two narrow white bands.*

HOUSEFLAG:

SERVICES: *Szczecin to London, Szczecin to Manchester, Liverpool Dublin, Belfast and Bristol Channel ports. (Cargo with limited passenger accommodation). Also world-wide services.*

Single-screw motorships with engines aft except those marked * which have engines amidships.

Boginka	...	...	498	**Nereida**	...	...	498	**Rokita**	...	...	492
Boruta	...	...	492	**Nimfa**	...	...	497	**Rusalka**	...	...	497
Dunajec	...	...	486	**Nogat**	...	...	620*	**San**	...	...	487*
Dziwozona	...	...	496	**Notec**	...	...	655*	**Skrzat**	...	...	496
Goplana	...	...	489	**Odra**	...	...	484	**Sola**	...	...	474
Ina	...	...	480	**Orla**	...	...	473	**Swietlik**	...	...	497
Kraznal	...	...	499	**Oksywie**	...	...	768*	**Syrenka**	...	...	497
Krutynia	...	...	473	**Pilica**	...	...	484	**Wila**	...	...	497
Ner	...	...	474	**Prosna**	...	...	615*	**Wodnica**	...	...	497

Also larger Ocean Freighters, etc.

Spain
CIA. MAR. GOLFO DE VIZCAYA, S.A.
BILBAO

FUNNEL:

HOUSEFLAG:

Alfonso Cuarto	...	...	...	1960	692	204	30	11	M(A)
Alfonso Tercero	...	...	...	1960	692	204	30	11	M(A)

NAVIERA LAGOS, S.A.
MADRID

FUNNEL: *Green with black top and large yellow letter "L".*

HOUSEFLAG:

Lago Como	...	...	...	...	1960	999	264	39	13½	M(A)
Lago Enol	...	...	...	...	1958	992	264	39	—	M(A)
Lago Garda	...	...	...	...	1960	999	264	39	—	M(A)
Lago Isoba	...	...	...	...	1958	992	260	37	11½	M(A)
Lago Mar	...	...	...	...	1923	1,502	268	38	12	SR
Lago Mayor	...	...	...	...	1922	1,499	267	38	12	SR
Lago Sanabria	...	...	...	...	1964	1,694	270	39	—	M

TRANSPORTES FRUTEROS DEL MEDITERRANEO, S.A.

VALENCIA

FUNNEL: *Yellow with black top and red and green houseflag.*

HOUSEFLAG: *Red over green pennant with black "T" on white disc.*

Amelia de Aspe	...	...	...	1956	689	222	37	—	M(A)
Glaciar Azul	...	...	...	1964	1,570	251	37	—	M(A)
Glaciar Blanco	...	...	...	1964	1,570	251	37	—	M(A)
Glaciar Gris ...	...	...	...	1965	1,570	251	37	—	M(A)
Glaciar Verde	...	...	...	1964	1,570	251	37	—	M(A)
Indunaval Primero...	...	...	1958	380	166	30	—	M(A)
Indunaval Tercero ...	...	...	1959	659	166	30	—	M(A)
Puerto de Burriana	...	...	1955	375	165	29	—	M(A)
Puerto de Cullera ...	...	...	1956	375	165	29	—	M(A)
Puerto de Denia	...	...	...	1955	375	165	29	—	M(A)

VASCO-MADRILENA DE NAVEGACION S.A.

BILBAO

FUNNEL: *Yellow with narrow black top and bold blue letters "V M".*

HOUSEFLAG:

Irus	...	...	...	...	1964	1,657	271	40	10	M(A)
Rio Hijuela	...	...	...	1960	1,642	261	39	10	M(A)
Tomas Ruiz de Velasco	...	...	1963	1,676	261	38	10	M(A)

Sweden

O. F. AHLMARK & CO. EFTR. A/B.

KARLSTAD

FUNNEL: *Black with black letter "A" on broad white band.*

HOUSEFLAG: *White pennant with black letter "A".*

Alstern	...	...	...	...	1957	499	244	34	12½	M(A)
Aspen ...	...	...	...	...	1964	499	244	34	12½	M(A)
Gapern	...	...	...	...	1952	1,520	285	36	—	M(A)
Immen	...	...	...	...	1950	1,500	285	41	11½	M
Noren	...	...	...	...	1958	2,352	286	42	11½	M
Racken	...	...	...	...	1960	488	222	30	—	M(A)
Saxen	...	...	...	...	1965	499	244	34	12½	M(A)
Silen	...	...	...	...	1948	1,376	237	36	11¼	M(A)
Skagern	...	...	...	...	1955	499	243	34	12½	M(A)
Toften	...	...	...	...	1958	354	196	31	—	M(A)
Visten	...	...	...	...	1960	747	255	36	11	M(A)

M.V. Silen. O. F. Ahlmark & Co. [*Fotoship*

M.V. Noren. O. F. Ahlmark & Co. [*John G. Callis*

M.V. Inga. A/B Transmarin. [*J. Clarkson*

AXEL F. ANDERSSON
HARNOSAND

FUNNEL: *Yellow with black top and yellow letter "N" on blue disc.*
HOUSEFLAG:

| Nordano | ... | ... | ... | ... | 1946 | 1,563 | 272 | 41 | — | SR |
| Ulvo ... | ... | ... | ... | ... | 1952 | 498 | 169 | 27 | 10 | M(A) |

STIG GORTHON
HELSINGBORG

FUNNEL: *White with black top and yellow monogram on blue disc.*
HOUSEFLAG: *White with yellow monogram on blue disc.*

Axel Gorthon	...	...	...	1955	2,121	315	44	14	M
Esbjorn Gorthon	...	...	...	1954	1,969	300	44	12½	M
Frans Gorthon	...	...	...	1956	1,962	315	44	13	M
Inga Gorthon	...	...	...	1951	1,959	332	45	14	M
Ingrid Gorthon	...	...	...	1952	1,959	332	45	14	M
Ivan Gorthon	...	...	...	1955	1,967	315	44	13½	M
Lovisa Gorthon	...	...	...	1953	2,112	315	44	13	M

Also larger Ocean Freighters.

IRIS REDERIAKTIEBOLAGET
STOCKHOLM

FUNNEL: *Black with white band. (Dark blue hulls).*
HOUSEFLAG: *Blue with large red letter "G".*

Jupiter	...	...	...	...	1936	1,553	310	44	9½	RT
Libra ...	...	...	...	...	1934	1,514	275	40	9	RT
Rigel ...	...	...	...	...	1938	2,400	346	46	14	M
Spica ...	...	...	...	...	1948	2,065	326	47	12	SR
Tauri ...	...	...	...	...	1949	2,334	336	47	11½	SR
Titan ...	...	...	...	...	1947	1,832	301	44	10½	SR
Virgo ...	...	...	...	...	1946	2,754	360	51	11½	RT

Atair and **Indus** are operated for an associated company.

ERIK KEKONIUS
GOTHENBURG

FUNNEL: *Black with red letter "B" on broad white band.*
HOUSEFLAG:

Brabantia	...	...	...	1965	500	—	—	—	M(A)
Flandria	...	...	...	1964	499	248	35	—	M(A)
Gertrud Bratt	...	...	...	1957	1,530	288	43	12	M
Nerlandia	...	...	...	1964	499	248	35	—	M(A)
Patria ...	...	...	...	1960	499	234	34	—	M(A)
Reine Astrid	...	...	...	1953	1,599	288	42	12	M

M.V. Irene. A/B Transmarin [*Fotoship*

M.V. Gertrude Bratt. Erik Kekonius. [*Fotoship*

M.V. Inga Gorthon. Stig Gorthon. [*Fotoship*

INGMAR MATSGARD
DALARO RED. A/B
STOCKHOLM

FUNNEL: *Black with broad yellow band.*

HOUSEFLAG:

Coastal Tankers:										
Sibris ...	...	...	...	...	1964	499	202	31	9½	M(A)
Sintus ...	...	...	...	...	1962	499	200	31	—	M(A)

STOCKHOLMS RED. "SVEA"
STOCKHOLM

FUNNEL: *Black with black letter "S" on broad white band.*

HOUSEFLAG: *White swallow tail with black letter "S" in centre and small Swedish ensign in top of hoist.*

Belos ...	...	...	...	...	1945	1,294	280	38	11½	SR
Bifrost	...	...	...	...	1945	1,574	292	40	12½	RT
Birger Jarl	...	...	...	...	1953	3,236	304	47	15	SR
Birka	...	...	...	...	1945	1,296	280	38	11½	SR
Brage ...	...	...	...	...	1937	1,344	273	38	10½	SR
Farida ...	...	...	...	...	1956	2,417	357	47	15	M
Fenris ...	...	...	...	...	1941	2,009	322	44	13	M
Fidra ...	...	...	...	...	1939	1,530	287	40	12	M
Finn ...	...	...	...	...	1920	1,599	286	41	8½	M(2A)
Fortuna ...	...	...	...	...	1955	2,410	357	47	15	M
Floria ...	...	...	...	...	1950	2,392	357	47	15	M
Freja ...	...	...	...	...	1938	1,503	287	40	13	M
Frey ...	...	...	...	...	1955	499	219	33	11½	M(A)
Froste ...	...	...	...	...	1945	1,924	322	44	13	M
Garm ...	...	...	...	...	1961	1,599	307	45	11½	M(A)
Grim ...	...	...	...	...	1961	1,599	307	45	11	M(A)
Hugin ...	...	...	...	...	1924	1,325	263	37	9½	SR
Loke ...	...	...	...	...	1957	499	219	33	11½	M(A)
Magne ...	...	...	...	...	1948	1,504	299	42	13	M
Mimer ...	...	...	...	...	1951	1,488	299	42	13	M
Mode ...	...	...	...	...	1949	1,478	299	42	13	M
Rote ...	...	...	...	...	1958	499	216	33	11½	M(A)
Stocksund	...	...	...	...	1959	2,934	375	51	—	M
Tor ...	...	...	...	...	1954	499	216	33	11½	M(A)

Also larger Ocean Freighters and Tankers.

RED. A/B SVENSKA LLOYD
GOTHENBURG

FUNNEL: *White with black top and yellow star on blue disc.*

HOUSEFLAG: *White with large blue Maltese cross.*

SERVICES: *Gothenburg to Tilbury (Passenger). Gothenburg and Swedish ports to London, Leith, Grangemouth, Methil, Newcastle and the Tyne, Sunderland, Liverpool and Manchester and the Mersey ports, etc. Swedish ports to European ports. (Cargo).*

Britannia	...	...	...	...	1929	4,652	376	50	17½	ST
Celia ...	...	...	...	...	1955	500	215	33	11½	M(A)

S.S. Jaroslaw Dadrowski. Polskie Linie.　　　　　　　[*John G. Callis*

M.V. Skrzat. Polska Zegluga.　　　　　　　[*D. Lynch*

M.V. Wila. Polska Zegluga.　　　　　　　[*Fotoship*

Hermia	...	...	...	...	1955	491	216	34	12	M(A)
Iberia	...	...	...	...	1903	1,432	249	35	9½	SR
Octavia	...	...	...	...	1958	499	218	33	12	M(A)
Portia	...	...	...	...	1955	493	216	33	12	M(A)
Silvia	...	...	...	...	1955	490	216	34	12	M(A)
Suecia	...	...	...	...	1929	4,661	376	50	17½	ST
Vinia	...	...	...	...	1958	500	218	33	12	M(A)

Other ships owned include: **Almeria, Begonia, Convallaria, Dalmatia, Gallia, Gandia, Hispania, Industria, Italia, Massilia, Scania, Scandinavia, Sicilia, Valencia, Valeria,** and **Venezia.** Also larger Ocean Freighters and Tankers.

A/B TRANSMARIN
ERIK LARSSON
HELSINGBORG

FUNNEL: *Black with large yellow letter "T".*
HOUSEFLAG: *Blue with large yellow letter "T".*

Becky	...	...	...	...	1945	1,792	326	44	13	M
Britta	...	...	...	...	1948	2,297	350	47	13	M
Eva Jeanette	...	...	...	...	1958	2,761	375	51	—	M(A)
Inga	...	...	...	...	1958	2,382	344	48	12¼	M
Irene	...	...	...	...	1956	1,820	329	44	13½	M
Kerstin	...	...	...	...	1956	2,308	361	48	12¾	M
Neva	...	...	...	...	1957	2,473	345	48	14	M(A)
Norma	...	...	...	...	1952	2,315	340	45	—	M
Siwa	...	...	...	...	1946	2,201	350	47	13	M
Ulla	...	...	...	...	1955	2,306	361	48	14¾	M
Ursa	...	...	...	...	1959	2,509	361	47	13½	M

Also larger Ocean Freighters.

U.S.S.R.

U.S.S.R. BALTIC STATE S.S. LINE

FUNNEL: *White with yellow hammer and sickle on red band. (Cargo ships, not listed: Black with yellow hammer and sickle on red band, or as above.)*

PASSENGER ROUTE: *London (and Havre) to Copenhagen, Gdynia, Stockholm, Helsinki and Leningrad.*

Baltika	...	...	...	...	1939	7,494	429*	60	20	TE(2)
Beloostrov	...	...	...	...	1937	2,916	295*	45	14	SR
Estonia	...	...	...	...	1960	4,722	401	53	18	M(2)
Mikhail Kalinin	...	...	...	...	1958	4,722	401	53	18	M(2)

All U.S.S.R. merchant ships are included in one comprehensive organisation covering world-wide services. It is not possible to list those units which regularly visit British ports.

BRITISH
TUGS

(Including Ocean Tugs based on the
nearer Continental Ports)

M.T. Vortex. Vokins & Co.

I. L. Bowen

INTRODUCTION

Tug design is highly specialised. The hull must be immensely strong and adequately protected by massive fenders to take hard knocks, the towing hook must be attached to a reinforced bulkhead or casing-end amidships and be placed as low as possible, thus necessitating curved "half-rounds" or towing rails over the after deck to prevent the towing rope fouling deck obstructions. The machinery must be equally powerful and many larger tugs and those for use in non-tidal waters are fitted with twin screws to afford greater manoeuvrability. Although the paddle tug has now almost disappeared from commercial service, this method of propulsion enabled very considerable turning force to be achieved when separately driven and for this reason new diesel-electric tugs with this form of propulsion have recently been delivered to the Admiralty.

Tugs may be broadly divided into the following categories:

1. **OCEAN SALVAGE TUGS** These are large units specially designed for extreme distances and may be engaged in bringing in a disabled vessel over many miles of ocean or for towing oil-drilling rigs or floating docks to places thousands of miles distant. Large bunkers are required and equipment must include wireless, lifeboats, fire-fighting and salvage apparatus. The Dutch have for long been pre-eminent in this field, although other European countries also have relatively large fleets. Opportunity has been taken in this edition to include lists of such fleets based on ports in Northern Europe from Cherbourg to Bremen which can occasionally be seen in this country. Tugs of this category are often based on ports far from their home harbours, although at the present time only the Overseas Towage & Salvage Co. from this country regularly stations tugs abroad.

2. **SHIP TOWAGE TUGS** Used in manoeuvring big ships in and out of docks, harbours, and estuaries, and occasionally employed on duties set out in paragraph 1 above. Again, a number of such tugs based on Continental ports and likely to be encountered on cross-channel journeys have been included, but it must be understood that limitations of space have restricted such entries to a selection of the larger companies.

3. **CRAFT TOWAGE and THAMES TUGS** Used for towing barges and lighters and to be seen in largest numbers on the Thames where some 8,000 barges are in use.

4. **LAUNCH TUGS, or "TOSHERS"** Used for manoeuvring barges in much the same way as Ship Towage Tugs handle larger ships. Although most commonly found on the Thames and in the London dock system, they are not restricted to these waters. Generally of under 40 tons gross, Launch Tugs are not generally included in this book although in the case of companies also operating larger vessels a mention of them is made in a footnote.

5. TENDER TUGS Generally large versions of Ship Towage tugs with the addition of considerable passenger accomodation which is indicated where figures are available.

This book begins with a general note on the tugs of the Admiralty and of a number of other operators who maintain tug fleets in more than one area, giving an indication in every case of the different ports where such vessels will be seen. Following this note, Tugs are for convenience arranged in ten areas, starting with the Thames and working clockwise round the coast of England and Scotland, following by Northern Ireland and Eire. An eleventh section deals with a selection of the larger European tug fleets based on ports from Cherbourg to Bremen. The areas are as follows :—

1   *Thames and Medway*

2   *South Coast (North Foreland to Lands End)*

3   *Bristol Channel and South Wales (Lands End to Milford Haven)*

4   *Mersey and Manchester*

5   *North West Coast (Formby Point to Portpatrick)*

6   *Clyde and West Coast of Scotland*

7   *East Coast of Scotland*

8   *North East Coast (Berwick to Flamborough Head)*

9   *Humber and East Coast*

10 *Northern Ireland and Eire*

11 *Northern Europe (Cherbourg to Bremen)*

February 1966   D.R.C.

General Note

The following operate Tug Fleets in more than one area, the Tugs being listed in their appropriate localities.

THE ADMIRALTY

FUNNEL: *Ocean Tugs : Grey, or grey with black top.*
Harbour Tugs : Yellow with black top. In certain cases a narrow coloured band indicates the department using them.

Note: There are no longer any Fleet Tugs (H.M. Ships) in service, all being now Royal Fleet Auxiliary, or Port Auxiliary Service units. Ocean Tugs have grey hulls, Harbour Tugs black.

PORTS: *Chatham, Portsmouth, Portland, Plymouth and Devonport, Pembroke, The Clyde, Rosyth and Londonderry.*
Further tugs are stationed abroad at Malta, Gibraltar, Singapore, and Hong Kong.

ALEXANDRA TOWING CO. LTD.

FUNNEL: *Yellow with black top separated by broad white band and narrow black ring.*

HOUSEFLAG: *White with red cross and red letters " A T C L " in each quarter.*

PORTS: *Southampton, Swansea, Port Talbot, and Liverpool.*

BRITISH RAILWAYS (British Transport Commission).

FUNNEL: *Red with black top and British Rail " twin-arrow " symbol in white. (Superseding yellow with black top)*

HOUSEFLAG: *Blue with white " twin-arrow " device.*

PORTS: *Newhaven, and Lowestoft.*

BRITISH TRANSPORT DOCKS (British Transport Commission).

FUNNEL: *South Wales : Black with narrow yellow band. Remainder Yellow with black top.*

HOUSEFLAG:

PORTS: *Newport, Cardiff and Barry, Fleetwood, Barrow-in-Furness, Hartlepool, Hull, and Grimsby.*

BRITISH WATERWAYS (British Transport Commission)

FUNNEL: *As listed under locality.*

HOUSEFLAG: *Blue with British Waterways device in yellow.*

PORTS: *Gloucester and Port Augustus. (British Waterways also operate small tugs, not listed, on the Aire & Calder Canal, River Humber, River Trent and Grand Union Canal.)*

R. & J. H. REA, LTD.

FUNNEL: *Red with black top, narrow white band and white " R " in a white bordered blue diamond.*

HOUSEFLAG: *Red with diamond design as on funnel.*

PORTS: *Southampton, Avonmouth, Cardiff and Milford Haven. (A similarly named and associated company, the Rea Towing Co. Ltd. operates a tug fleet at Liverpool)*

1. Thames & Medway

THAMES

W. H. J. ALEXANDER LTD. (SUN TUGS)

FUNNEL: *Black with broad red band, bordered by two narrow white bands.*

HOUSEFLAG: *Red with large white diamond and black " A ".*

Name					Date	Tons Gross	Horse Power	Engines
Sun II	...	...	...	...		Building		
Sun III	...	...	...	...		Building		
Sun IV	...	...	...	...	1915	200	750 (I)	SR
Sun V	...	...	...	...	1915	200	750 (I)	SR
Sun VIII	...	...	...	...	1919	196	750 (I)	SR
Sun X	...	...	...	...	1920	196	750 (I)	SR
Sun XII	...	...	...	...	1925	183	750 (I)	SR
Sun XV	...	...	...	...	1925	183	750 (I)	SR
Sun XVII	...	...	...	...	1946	233	1,030 (I)	SR
Sun XVIII	...	...	...	...	1951	105	640 (I)	M
Sun XIX	...	...	...	...	1956	175	1,210 (B)	M
Sun XX	...	...	...	...	1957	192	1,210 (B)	M
Sun XXI	...	...	...	...	1959	183	1,316 (B)	M
Sun XXII	...	...	...	...	1960	183	1,316 (B)	M
Sun XXIII	...	...	...	...	1961	150	1,400 (I)	M
Sun XXIV	...	...	...	...	1962	120	1,000 (I)	M
Sun XXV	...	...	...	...	1963	215	2,400 (I)	M
Sun XXVI	...	...	...	...	1964	215	2,400 (I)	M
Sunrise	...	...	...	...	1928	102	550 (I)	SR

ALPHA TOWAGE CO. LTD.

FUNNEL: *Black with " A " in white ring on red.*

HOUSEFLAG:

Alcydon ...	...	...	...	...	1937	39	280 (B)	M

Also the smaller tugs **Albraith** and **Algonda**.

ASSOCIATED PORTLAND CEMENT MANUFACTURERS LTD.

FUNNEL: *Black with white band bordered by blue and yellow bands with " Blue " on the upper and " Circle " on the lower.*

HOUSEFLAG:

Cemenco	...	...	...	...	1948	116	720 (B)	M
Cullamix	...	...	...	...	1938	96	650 (B)	M
Imperno	...	...	...	...	1935	38	200 (B)	M
Medusa								

W. T. BEAUMONT & SONS LTD.

FUNNEL: *Black with silver band and silver " B ".*
HOUSEFLAG: *Red with white letters " W T B & S " in white ring.*

Rodney II	...	...	...	...	1934		350	M

CHARRINGTON GARDNER LOCKET (LONDON) LTD.

FUNNEL: *Yellow with black top and blue band bordered by two narrow white bands.*
HOUSEFLAG: *Blue pennant with a white disc bearing a blue " C " and joined to each corner by a white stripe.*

Margaret Locket	...	...	...	1951	74	450 (B)	M
Charlock	...	...	...	1962	40	385 (B)	M

Also the smaller tugs **Miriam** and **Charlight**.

CLEMENTS, KNOWLING & CO. LTD.

FUNNEL: *Yellow with black top separated by narrow red band and with the monogram " JC " in red.*
HOUSEFLAG:

Ceekay	...	...	...	...	1930	37	400 (B)	M
Fenland ...	...	...	...	...	1929	38	400 (B)	M

WILLIAM CORY & SON, LTD.

FUNNEL: *Black with black diamond on broad white band.*
HOUSEFLAG: *Red with white diamond.*

Recruit ...	...	...	...	...	1952	91	670 (B)	M
Redoubt	...	...	...	...	1916	70	440 (B)	M
Relentless	...	...	...	...	1949	61	450 (B)	M
Revenge	...	...	...	...	1948	61	330 (B)	M

Also the launch tugs **Corcreek** and **Relay**

CORY TANK LIGHTERAGE LTD.

Funnel and Houseflag as above.

Crowstone	...	...	...	...	1932	48	330 (B)	M
Hawkstone	...	...	...	...	1948	61	450 (B)	M
Swiftstone	...	...	...	...	1952	91	670 (B)	M
Touchstone	...	...	...	...	1962	75		M

S.T. Seasider. Blyth Tug Co.
[*John G. Callis*

S.T. Watercock. Gamecock Tugs Ltd. [*R. Sherlock*

M.T. M.S.C. Ranger. Manchester Ship Canal Co.
[*Fotoship*

THE MERCANTILE LIGHTERAGE LTD.

Funnel and Houseflag as William Cory.

Breezy* ...	...	...	...	...	1914	71	390 (B)	M
Gusty† ...	...	...	...	...	1914	62	385 (B)	M
Hurricane	...	...	...	...	1938	90	550 (B)	M
Mersina ...	...	...	...	...	1955	79	670 (B)	M

Also the launch tugs **Cloudy, Hazy, Merano, Mercurian, Misty, Showery,** and **Squally.**
*Rebuilt. †Rebuilt 1954.

W. R. CUNIS LTD.

FUNNEL : *White with black top and broad red band separated by narrow white band.*

HOUSEFLAG :

William Ryan* ...	...	...	...	—	72	530 (B)	M

Also the small tug **Wal.** *Rebuilt 1956.

W. J. EARNELL & SONS.

FUNNEL : *Red with black top separated by white band.*

HOUSEFLAG :

The small tugs **Constance, General II,** and **Porpoise.**

ERITH & DARTFORD LIGHTERAGE CO. LTD.

FUNNEL :

HOUSEFLAG :

Caroline	...	...	...	...	1937	50	340 (B)	M

ERITH TOWING CO. LTD.

FUNNEL : *Red with black top separated by narrow white band and with white letters " ETC ".*

HOUSEFLAG :

Herbert Clarke	...	...	...	1948	45	250 (B)	M

Also the smaller Launch tug **Morland.**

ESSO PETROLEUM CO. LTD

FUNNEL: *Black with " Esso " in red in blue ring on broad white band.*

HOUSEFLAG: *White with " Esso " in red in blue ring.*

Esso Greenwich	...	...	...	1953	77	550 (B)	M
Esso Reading	...	...	...	1954	77	550 (B)	M

F. T. EVERARD & SONS LTD.

FUNNEL: *Black with houseflag.*

HOUSEFLAG: *Quartered diagonally white above and below two red quarters.*

E. A. Everard	...	...	...	1943	54	400 (B)	M
P. S. Everard	...	...	...	1944	54	220 (I)	SR
S. A. Everard	...	...	...	1939	124	800 (B)	M

Also the smaller launch tugs **Jester** and **Joker**. The company also operates a large fleet of coasters.

F. G. TOWING CO. LTD.

FUNNEL: *Black with blue disc bearing the red letters " FG ".*

HOUSEFLAG:

The small launch tugs **Efgee,** and **Dancha.**

W. J. WOODWARD FISHER.

FUNNEL: *White with white " F " on black band.*

HOUSEFLAG: *White with blue cross and blue letters " W J W F ", one in each quarter.*

The small motor tugs **Duke Shore** and **Plodder,** and the launch tugs **Awlot, Billdora, Ikangoit, Ikanopit, Kando, Opabout, Opon, Otazel,** and **Willdo.**

FLOWER & EVERETT, LTD.

FUNNEL: *Yellow with broad red band.*

HOUSEFLAG:

Bankside	...	...	...	...	1944	—	500 (B)	M
Chelsea ...	...	...	...	...	1940	67	500 (B)	M
Grosvenor	...	...	...	...	1912	56	480 (B)	M
Tudorose	...	...	...	...	1936	—	580 (B)	M
Vange	...	...	...	...	1936	—	375 (B)	M

M.T. Sun XXI. W.
H. J. Alexander.
[*R. Sherlock*

M.T. S. A. Everard.
F. T. Everard &
Sons.
[*John G. Callis*

M.T. Bankside
Flower & Everett.
[*A. Duncan*

GASELEE & SON LTD.

FUNNEL: *Buff with three red rings.*

HOUSEFLAG: *Yellow swallowtail with red border at top and bottom and a red stripe through centre with blue letters " G & S ".*

Aboma	...	...	...	...	...	1933	67	450 (B)	M
Agama	...	...	...	...	...	1937	84	500 (B)	M
Culex	...	...	...	...	...	1958	98	660 (B)	M
Fossa	...	...	...	...	...	1961	83	1,000 (B)	M
Gnat	...	...	...	...	...	1934	66	390 (B)	M
Mamba	...	...	...	...	...	1935	66	390 (B)	M
Naja	...	...	...	...	...	1936	52	300 (B)	M
Rana	...	...	...	...	...	1951	99	700 (B)	M
Tayra	...	...	...	...	...	1926	106	700 (B)	M
Vespa	...	...	...	...	...	1934	92	520 (B)	M

Also the smaller motor tugs **Asp** and **Boa**.

GENERAL STEAM NAVIGATION CO. LTD.

FUNNEL: *Black with replica of houseflag.*

HOUSEFLAG: *White with red globe over the date " 1824 " in the centre and the red letters " G. S. N. C. " in each corner.*

Gull	...	...	...	...	...	1952	75	310 (B)	M

Owners of a large fleet of Coastal and Short Sea vessels.

GREENHITHE LIGHTERAGE CO. LTD.

FUNNEL: *Yellow.*

HOUSEFLAG:

(These tugs are distinguished by green hulls)

Britannia*	...	...	...	...	1893	76	360 (B)	M

Also the smaller tugs **Calliope, Hermoine** and **Leonie**.
*Rebuilt.

HARRISONS (LONDON) LTD.

FUNNEL: *Black with diagonal black stripes on broad white band.*

HOUSEFLAG:

Birchrock	...	...	...	...	1959	37	560 (B)	M

JOHN HAWKINS LTD.

FUNNEL: *White with red pyramid.*

HOUSEFLAG:

John Hawkins ...	...	...	...	1946	50	275 (B)	M

Also the smaller Launch Tug **Rosemau**.

HUMPHREY & GREY (LIGHTERAGE) LTD.

FUNNEL: *Black with broad band bordered by two narrow white bands.*
HOUSEFLAG: *Blue with a yellow Maltese Cross in a red ring.*

Flanchford	...	...	...	...	1921	51	320 (B)	M
Friston Down	...	...	...	...	1964	80	—	M
Owen Smith	...	...	...	...	1946	66	450 (B)	M
Rocott	...	...	...	...	1921	58	350 (B)	M
St. Aubrey	...	...	...	...	1962	—	—	M
St. Olaf	...	...	...	...	1956	37	360 (B)	M
Scottie	...	...	...	...	1930	50	270 (B)	M

Also the smaller Launch Tug **Fortune**

J. P. KNIGHT LTD.
J. P. KNIGHT (LONDON) LTD., AND COOK & TESTER LTD.

FUNNEL: *Black with two silver bands above silver " K ".*
HOUSEFLAG:

Kara	...	...	...	...	1935	56	390 (B)	M
Kathleen	...	...	...	...	1936	47	260 (B)	M
Katra	...	...	...	...	1936	68	520 (B)	M
Kawara	...	...	...	...	1934	74	455 (B)	M
Kelpy	...	...	...	...	1934	48	300 (B)	M
Kemsing	...	...	...	...	1960	135	1,100 (B)	M
Kendal	...	...	...	...	1940	230	1,160 (B)	M
Kenley	...	...	...	...	1958	246	1,500 (B)	M
Kent	...	...	...	...	1948	121	880 (B)	M
Keston	...	...	...	...	1940	41	300 (B)	M
Kestrel	...	...	...	...	1955	223	1,150 (B)	M
Keverne	...	...	...	...	1960	260	1,650 (B)	M
Khurdah	...	...	...	...	1930	50	495 (B)	M
Kite	...	...	...	...	1952	118	960 (B)	M
Kundah	...	...	...	...	1939	69	520 (B)	M

Also the smaller tugs **Forceful, Greenhythe, Medway Fearnought** and **Stone**.
Tugs are also stationed at Rochester and Sheerness.

LONDON & ROCHESTER TRADING CO. LTD.

FUNNEL: *Black with silver crescent on broad red band between two narrow white bands.*
HOUSEFLAG: *Red with silver crescent.*
(These vessels have light brown hulls).

Dragette	...	...	...	...	1947	50	300 (B)	M

Also the smaller tugs **Coaxette, Nudgette, Shovette** and **Snatchette**.

M.T. Mamba. Gase-
lee & Sons.
  [*D. R. Chesterton*

M.T. Gull. General
Steam Navigation
Co.
  [*D. R. Chesterton*

S.T. Danube VIII.
London Dredging
Co.
  [*John G. Callis*

LONDON DREDGING CO. LTD.
LATE TILBURY CONTRACTING & DREDGING CO. LTD.

FUNNEL: *Black with houseflag.*
HOUSEFLAG: *Divided diagonally from top of hoist, yellow over blue.*

Danube IV	...	...	...	...	1927	266	829 (I)	SR
Danube V	...	...	...	...	1935	241	900 (I)	SR
Danube VI	...	...	...	...	1935	241	900 (I)	SR
Danube VII	...	...	...	...	1946	237	900 (I)	SR
Danube VIII	...	...	...	...	1946	237	900 (I)	SR

Also the smaller tug **Pullwell**.

MERCANTILE LIGHTERAGE CO. LTD.

See Wm. Cory & Son Ltd.

NORTH THAMES GAS BOARD

FUNNEL: *Black with band of red pyramids over two narrow black bands, all on a broad white band.*
HOUSEFLAG: *White, with a red rising sun device in the centre and the blue letters " N T G B " in each corner.*

Beckton II	...	...	...	...	1957	43	202 (B)	M Kort Nozzle

Also the smaller tug **Barking**

R. G. ODELL LTD.

FUNNEL: *Black with blue " O " on broad white band.*
HOUSEFLAG: *White pennant with blue border and blue " O " in centre.*

Churchill*	...	...	...	...	1910	70	480 (B)	M

Also the smaller tugs **Leo, Oasis, Oxford, Rennie, Walton, Winston** and **Union**.
*Rebuilt in 1953.

G. J. PALMER & SONS.

FUNNEL: *Blue with red top separated by a black band bordered by narrow white bands.*

HOUSEFLAG:

Radio ...	...	...	...	...	—	—	180 (B)	M
Sir Montagu	...	...	...	...	1936	61	440 (B)	M

Also the smaller tugs **Ansay** and **London Pioneer**.

A. H. GREEN & CO. LTD.

Funnel and Houseflag as G. J. Palmer & Son.

| Premiere | ... | ... | ... | ... | 1929 | 38 | 200 (B) | M |
| Tat | ... | ... | ... | ... | 1930 | 51 | 270 (B) | M |

T. H. PEARCE

FUNNEL:

HOUSEFLAG:

| Jolly Tar | ... | ... | ... | ... | 1926 | 34 | 100 (B) | M |

PORT OF LONDON AUTHORITY

FUNNEL: *Yellow, or Yellow with black top.*

HOUSEFLAG: *White with red St. George's cross with P.L.A. arms at centre.*

River Tugs:

Lord Devonport	...	...	...	1959	130	935 (B)	M
Lord Ritchie	...	...	...	1960	130	935 (B)	M
Lord Waverley	...	...	...	1960	130	935 (B)	M
Mardyke	...	...	...	1957	37	302 (B)	M
Thorney	...	...	...	1943	137	500 (I)	SR
Westbourne	...	...	...	1912	185	575 (I)	SR

Dock Tugs:

Beam	...	...	...	...	1910	168	1,000 (B)	SR(2)
Brent	...	...	...	...	1946	54	220 (I)	SR
Deanbrook	...	...	...	1946	54	220 (I)	SR
Dollar Bay	...	...	...	1944	54	220 (I)	SR
Lea	...	...	...	...	1946	54	220 (I)	SR
Placard*	...	...	...	—	122	1,600 (B)	M
Plaboy	...	...	...	...	1957	36	360 (B)	M
Plagal	...	...	...	...	1951	159	1,200 (B)	M
Plangent...	...	...	...	1951	159	1,200 (B)	M
Plankton*	...	...	...	—	122	1,600 (B)	M
Plasma* ...	...	...	...	—	122	1,600 (B)	M
Plastron	...	...	...	1953	80	400 (B)	M
Plateau ...	...	...	...	1952	159	1,200 (B)	M
Platina ...	...	...	...	1952	159	1,200 (B)	M
Platoon*...	...	...	...	—	122	1,600 (B)	M

Also the smaller tugs **Malta, Placate, Plashy, Plaudit,** and **Velox,** and a large fleet of harbour and salvage vessels, etc.

*Building.

RIVER LIGHTERAGE CO. LTD.
STEPHENSON CLARKE, LTD.

FUNNEL: *Yellow with black top separated by red band.*

HOUSEFLAG: *None.*

| Brent Brook | ... | ... | ... | ... | 1948 | 68 | 520 (B) | M |
| Falcon Brook | ... | ... | ... | 1956 | 58 | 310 (B) | M |

M.T. Plagal. Port of London Authority.
[*John G. Callis*

M.T. Flying Cock. North West Tugs Ltd.   [*J. Clarkson*

M.T. M.S.C. Sovereign.   Manchester Ship Canal Co.
[*J. Clarkson*

SILVERTOWN SERVICES LIGHTERAGE LTD.

FUNNEL: *Black with two blue bands alternating between three silver bands.*
HOUSEFLAG: *Two horizontal blue bands on silver field.*

Silverbeam	...	...	...	...	1951	92	605 (B)	M
Silverdial	...	...	...	...	1950	92	605 (B)	M
Silverlane*	...	...	...	...	1925	103	480 (B)	M
Silvermark	...	...	...	...	1937	88	500 (B)	M
Silvertown	...	...	...	...	1940	83	520 (B)	M

Also the smaller Launch Tugs **Silverlit, Silverdash** and **Silverdot.**
*Rebuilt in 1953.

THAMES CONSERVANCY

FUNNEL: *Cream.*
HOUSEFLAG: *White with red St. George's cross with T.C.C. arms at centre.*

| Wey | ... | ... | ... | ... | ... | 1939 | — | — | M |
| Bourne | ... | ... | ... | ... | ... | 1939 | — | — | M |

These tugs operate on the upper reaches of the Thames.

THAMES & GENERAL LIGHTERAGE LTD.

FUNNEL: *Blue with red top and large white letter " T ".*
HOUSEFLAG: *Divided horizontally red over blue with large white letter " T ".*

General IV	...	...	...	...	1936	50	390 (B)	M
General VI	...	...	...	...	—	—	—	M
General VII	...	...	...	...	1962	63	665 (B)	M
Irande*	...	...	...	...	1929	96	350 (B)	M
Robertsbridge†	...	...	...	...	1937	90	450 (B)	M
Wortha†	...	...	...	...	1929	96	405 (B)	M

Also the smaller Launch Tugs **Blackboys, Brent Lee, Eager, Endeavour, Energetic, Ensign, Express, Glen Lee, Jane Lee, Nancy Lee, Thorn Lee** and **Tommy Lee II.**
*Re-engined 1947.   †Re-engined 1962.

TILBURY CONTRACTING & DREDGING CO. LTD.

See London Dredging Co. Ltd.

TOUGH & HENDERSON

FUNNEL: *Yellow with two red rings.*
HOUSEFLAG: *Yellow pennant bordered by two red lines and with red letters " T & H ".*

| Ham* | ... | ... | ... | ... | ... | 1925 | 44 | 240 (B) | SR |
| Sheen* | ... | ... | ... | ... | ... | 1925 | 52 | 300 (B) | M |

Also the smaller tug **Teddington.**   *Rebuilt in 1961 and 1958 respectively.

UNION LIGHTERAGE CO. LTD.

FUNNEL: *Black*

HOUSEFLAG: *Blue with white lettering " Union Lighterage Co. Ltd. "*

Banco	...	...	...	...	1927	107	535 (B)	SR
Broncho	...	...	...	...	1922	69	250 (B)	SR
Hembo	...	...	...	...	1953	80	560 (B)	M
Lectro	...	...	...	...	1933	120	720 (B)	ME
Lingo	...	...	...	...	1964	83	627 (B)	M
Rio	...	...	...	...	1934	80	310 (B)	M
Rodeo	...	...	...	...	1924	37	120 (B)	M
Trinco	...	...	...	...	1945	77	480 (B)	M
Unico	...	...	...	...	1927	51	200 (B)	M

Also the smaller Launch Tug **Vago.**

The company also operates a fleet of river tankers.

VOKINS & CO. LTD.

FUNNEL: *Dark blue with red " V " on white disc.*

HOUSEFLAG: *None.*

Vanoc	...	...	...	...	1937	58	390 (B)	M
Vista	...	...	...	...	1940	71	420 (B)	M
Voracious*	...	...	...	...	1929	64	500 (B)	M
Vortex	...	...	...	...	1947	77	465 (B)	M

Also the smaller Launch Tugs **Valkrie, Vampire, Varlet,** and **Vassal.**

*Rebuilt 1960.

WILLIAM WATKINS LTD. (SHIP TOWAGE LTD.)

FUNNEL: *Black with broad red band over a narrow blue band with the houseflag thereon.*

HOUSEFLAG: *Red swallowtail with large white " W ".*

Atlantic Cock	...	...	...	...	1932	182	1,000 (I)	SR
Avenger	...	...	...	...	1962	300	2,250 (I)	M
Cervia	...	...	...	...	1946	233	900 (I)	SR
Challenge	...	...	...	...	1931	212	1,150 (I)	SR
Contest	...	...	...	...	1933	213	1,150 (I)	SR
Crested Cock	...	...	...	...	1935	177	1,000 (I)	SR
Dhulia	...	...	...	...	1959	272	2,000 (I)	M
Gondia	...	...	...	...	1927	200	850 (I)	SR
Hibernia	...	...	...	...	1962	350	2,250 (I)	M
Ionia	...	...	...	...	1960	120	1,200 (I)	M
Java	...	...	...	...	1905	128	500 (I)	SR
Moorcock	...	...	...	...	1959	273	2,000 (I)	M
Muria	...	...	...	...	1932	165	850 (I)	SR
Napia	...	...	...	...	1943	261	1,200 (I)	SR
Ocean Cock	...	...	...	...	1932	182	1,000 (I)	SR
Racia	...	...	...	...	1930	163	850 (I)	SR
Tanga	...	...	...	...	1931	203	850 (I)	SR
Vanquisher	...	...	...	...	1955	294	1,900 (I)	M
Watercock	...	...	...	...	1923	200	750 (I)	SR

M.T. Dhulia. William Watkins Ltd.
[*R. Sherlock*

S.T. Knocker White.
W. E. White & Sons.
[*D. R. Chesterton*

S.T. Tanga. William Watkins Ltd.
[*D. R. Chesterton*

W. E. WHITE & SONS

FUNNEL: *Black with white " W ".*

HOUSEFLAG: *Royal blue with large white " W ".*

Doris White	...	...	...	...	1930	40	500	M
Knocker White		...	...	...	1924	96	—	M
Lily White	...	...	...	...	1929	38	300 (B)	M
Louisa White		...	...	...	1949	39	300 (B)	M
Sarah White	...	...	...	...	1925	34	280 (B)	M
William White		...	...	...	1915	30	120 (B)	M

W. J. R. WHITEHAIR, LTD.

FUNNEL: *Yellow with black top and red " G Q ".*

HOUSEFLAG:

The small tugs **Charles W., Kenneth G., Sidney G.** and **William J.**

SAMUEL WILLIAMS & SONS LTD.
DAGENHAM LIGHTERAGE, LTD.

FUNNEL: *Black with broad blue band.*

HOUSEFLAG: *None.*

Arthur	...	...	...	...	1957	50	460 (B)	M
Barroness	...	...	...	...	1950	72	450 (B)	M
Princess	...	...	...	...	1949	72	450 (B)	M
Varco	...	...	...	...	1957	50	460 (B)	M

Also the smaller Launch Tugs **Gipsy, Jaymar** and **Sullivan.**

A number of other Thames tug companies operate small Launch Tugs.

CHATHAM
THE ADMIRALTY

FUNNEL: *See General Note at the beginning of this section.*

Harbour Tugs:

Betty	...	...	...	...	1963	38	400	M
Chainshot	...	...	...	...	1945	56	350	M
Collie	...	...	...	...	1964	152	1,320	M(2)
Expeller	...	...	...	...	1942	317	820	M
Grapeshot	...	...	...	...	1945	57	350	M
Prompt	...	...	...	...	1943	232	900	SR
Resolve	...	...	...	...	1946	290	800	SR
T.I.D. 107	...	...	...	...	1943	55	220	SR
T.I.D. 172	...	...	...	...	1943	55	220	SR

MEDWAY

Units of the fleets of the Associated Portland Cement Manufacturers Ltd., Wm. Cory & Son Ltd. and their associated companies, Gaselee & Son Ltd., J. P. Knight Ltd., and the London & Rochester Trading Co. Ltd. regularly operate on and from the Medway.

2. South Coast

DOVER HARBOUR BOARD

FUNNEL: *None.*

HOUSEFLAG: *Blue with the Arms of the Cinque Ports in full colour surrounded by the inscription " DOVER HARBOUR BOARD 1606 ".*

| Diligent ... | ... | ... | ... | ... | 1957 | 161 | 1,040 (B) | M(2) |
| Dominant | ... | ... | ... | ... | 1958 | 161 | 1,040 (B) | M(2) |

BRITISH RAILWAYS

FUNNEL and HOUSEFLAG: *See General Note at the beginning of this section.*

| Meeching | ... | ... | ... | ... | 1960 | 160 | — | M(2) |

SHOREHAM HARBOUR TRUSTEES

FUNNEL: *Black.*

HOUSEFLAG:

| Kingston Buci ... | ... | ... | ... | 1960 | 70 | — | M |

THE ADMIRALTY

FUNNEL: *See General Note at the beginning of this section.*

Ocean Tugs:

Agile ...	...	...	...	...	1958	641	1,600	M(2)
Cyclone ...	...	...	...	...	1943	1,100	3,020	M(2)
Reward ...	...	...	...	...	1945	1,136	3,020	M(2)
Typhoon	...	...	...	...	1959	1,100	2,750	M

Harbour Tugs:

Alice ...	...	...	...	...	1961	38	400	M
Boxer ...	...	...	...	...	1963	152	1,320	M(2)
Bridget ...	...	...	...	...	1963	38	400	M
Cannon ...	...	...	...	...	1944	122	400	SR
Capable ...	...	...	...	...	1946	832	3,000	SR(2)
Confiance	...	...	...	...	1956	641	1,600	M(2)
Eminent	...	...	...	...	1946	295	800	SR

Forceful ...	...	...	...	...	1957	473	1,600	ME(PW)
Grinder ...	...	...	...	...	1958	473	1,600	ME(PW)
Regard ...	...	...	...	...	1938	144	520	SR
Samson ...	...	...	...	...	1954	855	3,000	(SR 2)
T.I.D. 3 ...	...	...	...	...	1944	55	220	SR
T.I.D. 32	...	...	...	...	1943	55	220	SR
T.I.D. 99	...	...	...	...	1943	55	220	SR

CORRALL, LTD.
LATE FRASER & WHITE LTD.

FUNNEL: *Yellow with black top separated by narrow white band.*

HOUSEFLAG:

Industrious	...	...	...	...	1944	55	—	M

Also the smaller tug **Zealous.**

SOUTHAMPTON
ALEXANDRA TOWING CO. LTD.

FUNNEL and HOUSEFLAG: *See General Note at beginning of this section.*

Brockenhurst ...	...	...	...	1964	174	1,200 (B)	M
Canada ...	...	...	...	...	1951	237	1,200 (I)	SR
Flying Breeze*...	...	...	...	1938	460	1,000 (I)	SR
Gladstone	...	...	...	...	1951	237	1,200 (I)	SR
North Isle	...	...	...	...	1959	200	1,350 (B)	M
North Loch	...	...	...	...	1959	200	1,350 (B)	M
Romsey ...	...	...	...	...	1964	174	1,200 (B)	M
Ventnor ...	...	...	...	...	1965	174	1,200 (B)	M

Also tug fleets at Liverpool, Swansea and Port Talbot.   *Tender, 250 passengers.

JAMES CONTRACTING & SHIPPING CO. LTD.

FUNNEL: *White with black top.*

HOUSEFLAG: *Blue swallowtail with large white " J " (Alternatively, a flag divided diagonally from the top of hoist, yellow over blue)*

Hauler ...	...	...	...	...	1926	143	240 (I)	M
Jumsey ...	...	...	...	...	1928	30	180 (B)	M
Tideall ...	...	...	...	...	1943	54	336	SR
Tideway	...	...	...	...	1944	54	336	SR

M.T. Reward. The
Admiralty.
 [*D. R. Chesterton*

M.T. Dominant.
Dover Harbour
Board.
 [*John G. Callis*

S.T. Canute. South-
ampton I.O.W. & S.
of E.S.P. Co.
 [*D. R. Chesterton*

R. & J. H. REA, LTD.

FUNNEL and HOUSEFLAG: *See General Note at the beginning of this section.*

| Testgarth | ... | ... | ... | ... | 1937 | 60 | 390 (B) | M |

Also tug fleets at Avonmouth, Milford Haven, Cardiff and Barry.

SOUTHAMPTON, ISLE OF WIGHT & SOUTH OF ENGLAND STEAM PACKET CO. LTD.

FUNNEL: *Dark red with black top.*

HOUSEFLAG: *Quartered diagonally; white, blue, green, red.*

Atherfield	...	...	...	...	1956	253	1,340 (B)	M(2)
Calshot*	...	...	...	...	1964	475	1,800 (B)	M(2)
Canute	...	...	...	...	1923	271	1,200 (I)	SR(2)
Chale	...	...	...	...	(Building)			
Clausentum	...	...	...	...	1926	268	1,200 (I)	SR(2)
Culver	...	...	...	...	1956	246	1,340 (B)	M(2)
Dunnose	...	...	...	...	1958	241	1,340 (B)	M(2)
Gatcombe*	...	...	...	...	1960	475	1,800 (B)	M(2)
Hamtun	...	...	...	...	1953	318	1,500 (I)	SR(2)
Sir Bevois	...	...	...	...	1953	318	1,500 (I)	SR(2)
Thorness	...	...	...	...	1953	318	1,340 (B)	M(2)

*Tenders, each with accommodation for 400 passengers (200 between ship and shore).

POOLE HARBOUR
HARRY ROSE (TOWAGE) LTD.

FUNNEL: *Red with black top and white " H R " in white ring.*

HOUSEFLAG:

Wendy Ann	...	...	...	...	1950	29	350 (I)	M
Wendy Ann 2	...	...	...	...	1940	44	500 (I)	M

PORTLAND
THE ADMIRALTY

FUNNEL: *See General Note at the beginning of this section.*

Harbour Tugs:

Agatha	...	...	...	...	...	1961	38	400	M
Agnes	...	...	...	...	...	1961	38	400	M
Antic	...	...	...	...	...	1943	630	1,350	SR
Beagle	...	...	...	...	...	1963	152	1,320	M(2)
T.I.D. 68	...	...	...	...	...	1944	55	220	SR

THE ADMIRALTY

FUNNEL: *See General Note at the beginning of this section.*

Ocean Tugs:

Bustler ...	...	...	...	...	1942	1,100	3,020	M(2)
Samsonia	...	...	...	...	1942	1,100	3,020	M(2)

Harbour Tugs:

Accord ...	...	...	...	...	1958	641	1,600	M(2)
Alsatian	...	...	...	...	1961	152	1,320	M(2)
Audrey ...	...	...	...	...	1961	38	400	M
Bombshell	...	...	...	...	1945	56	350	M
Brenda ...	...	...	...	...	1963	38	400	M
Careful	...	...	...	...	1946	832	3,000	SR(2)
Faithful ...	...	...	...	...	1957	473	1,600	ME(PW)
Favourite	...	...	...	...	1958	473	1,600	ME(PW)
Foremost	...	...	...	...	1938	143	500	SR
Superman	...	...	...	...	1954	855	3,000	SR

W. J. REYNOLDS, LTD.

FUNNEL: *Yellow with black top.*

HOUSEFLAG:

Anthony	...	...	...	...	1902	115	585 (I)	SR
Bahia ...	...	...	...	...	1907	86	350 (I)	SR
Carbeile	...	...	...	...	1929	110	350 (I)	SR
Tactful ...	...	...	...	...	1909	112	400 (I)	SR
Trevol ...	...	...	...	...	1921	137	650 (I)	M

Also the smaller tug **Wolsdon.**

FOWEY HARBOUR COMMISSIONERS

FUNNEL: *Yellow with black top*

HOUSEFLAG: *None.*

Cannis ...	...	...	...	...	1953	91	600 (B)	M
St. Canute	...	...	...	...	1931	139	500 (I)	SR

FALMOUTH DOCKS & ENGINEERING CO. LTD.

FUNNEL: *Red with black top.*

HOUSEFLAG: *None.*

Portwey	...	...	...	...	1927	94	330 (I)	SR

M.T. Gatcombe.
Southampton
I.O.W. & S. of
E.S.P. Co.
        [*R. Sherlock*

M.T. Wendy Ann 3.
H. Rose (Towage)
Ltd.   [*H. Rose*

S.T. St. Mawes.
Falmouth Towage
Co.   [*J. Clarkson*

FALMOUTH TOWAGE CO. LTD.

FUNNEL: *Black with broad white band.*

HOUSEFLAG: *None.*

(These tugs have black over green hulls)

Lynch	...	...	...	...	1924	211	650 (I)	SR
St. Agnes	...	...	...	...	1925	226	678 (I)	SR
St. Denys	...	...	...	...	1929	174	790 (I)	SR
St. Just	...	...	...	...	1957	62	—	M
St. Levan	...	...	...	...	1942	160	700 (I)	SR
St. Mawes	...	...	...	...	1951	346	800 (I)	SR
St. Merryn	...	...	...	...	1945	233	1,000 (I)	SR

3. Bristol Channel and South Wales

BRISTOL AND AVONMOUTH

F. A. ASHMEAD & SON, LTD.

FUNNEL: *Black with red " A " on broad white band between two narrow red bands.*

HOUSEFLAG: *White pennant with red " A ".*

The small tugs **Robert A., Hubert A.,** and **Judith A.**

BRISTOL DOCKS AUTHORITY

FUNNEL: *Black with a band of red squares superimposed on a broader white band.*

HOUSEFLAG:

Cabot	...	...	...	...	1952	98	—	M

T. R. BROWN & SONS LTD.

FUNNEL: *Black with broad red band between two silver bands.*
HOUSEFLAG: *White with black bordered red diamond containing black " B ".*

| Ernest Brown ... | ... | ... | ... | 1944 | 54 | — | M |

Also the smaller tugs **Leader** and **Medway**.

C. J. KING & SONS LTD.

FUNNEL: *White with black top separated by broad red band.*
HOUSEFLAG: *Red with white diamond containing black " K ".*

Bristolian	...	...	...	...	1911	174	—	SR
John King	...	...	...	...	1936	49	300 (B)	M
Sea Alarm	...	...	...	...	1941	263	1,000 (I)	SR
Sea Alert	...	...	...	...	1960	120	630 (B)	M
Sea Gem	...	...	...	...	1944	54	220 (I)	SR
Sea Merrimac	...	...	...	...	1964	170	850 (B)	M
Sea Queen	...	...	...	...	1944	244	1,000 (I)	SR
Sea Volunteer	...	...	...	...	1962	170	850 (B)	M

R. & J. H. REA, LTD.

FUNNEL and HOUSEFLAG: *See General Note at the beginning of this section.*

Avongarth	...	...	...	...	1960	156	805 (B)	M
Falgarth	...	...	...	...	1958	102	500 (B)	M
								Kort Nozzle
Pengarth	...	...	...	...	1962	160	1,080 (B)	M
Polgarth	...	...	...	...	1962	160	1,080 (B)	M

Also tugs at Southampton, Cardiff, Barry and Milford Haven.

GLOUCESTER
BRITISH WATERWAYS

FUNNEL: *Black with broad yellow band.*
HOUSEFLAG: *Blue with yellow British Waterways device (Blue over black hulls)*

Addie	...	...	...	...	1915	48	360 (B)	M
Primrose	...	...	...	...	1906	52	180 (I)	SR
Resolute	...	...	...	...	1897	64	—	M
Severn Iris	...	...	...	...	—	51	240 (B)	M
Severn Victor	...	...	...	...	1904	44	204 (B)	M
Stanegarth	...	...	...	...	1910	47	—	M

Also the smaller tugs **Severn Enterprise** and **Severn Progress**.

BRITISH TRANSPORT DOCKS

FUNNEL and HOUSEFLAG: *See General Note at the beginning of this section.*

Llanwern	...	...	...	...	1960	160	1,200 (B)	M
Newport	...	...	...	...	1956	139	700 (B)	M
St. Woolas	...	...	...	...	1960	160	1,200 (B)	M

May also work from Cardiff or other South Wales ports.

NEWPORT SCREW TOWING CO. LTD.

FUNNEL: *Black with two narrow white bands.*

HOUSEFLAG:

Duncurlew	...	...	...	...	1962	190	—	M
Dunfalcon	...	...	...	...	1941	252	1,000 (I)	SR
Dunhawk	...	...	...	...	1943	244	1,000 (I)	SR
Dunsnipe	...	...	...	...	1962	190	—	M

CARDIFF AND BARRY

R. & J. H. REA, LTD.

FUNNEL and HOUSEFLAG: *See General Note at the beginning of this section.*

Exegarth	...	...	...	...	1942	173	750 (I)	SR
Hallgarth	...	...	...	...	1943	203	650 (I)	SR
Iselgarth	...	...	...	...	1949	152	810 (I)	SR
Lowgarth*	...	...	...	...	1965	155	850 (B)	M
Nethergarth	...	...	...	...	1931	150	800 (I)	SR
Plumgarth	...	...	...	...	1960	156	805 (B)	M
Tregarth*	...	...	...	...	1958	102	500 (B)	M
Westgarth	...	...	...	...	1954	262	1,000 (I)	SR
Yewgarth	...	...	...	...	1945	274	850 (I)	SR

Also tug fleets at Southampton, Avonmouth and Milford Haven.

* Kort Nozzle.

ALEXANDRA TOWING CO. LTD.

FUNNEL and HOUSEFLAG: *See General Note at the beginning of this section.*

Brambles	...	...	...	...	1942	242	1,100 (I)	SR
Caswell ...	...	...	...	...	1943	276	850 (I)	SR
Flying Kestrel ...	...	...	...	1943	244	1,100 (I)	SR
Margam	...	...	...	...	1930	187	750 (I)	SR
Mumbles	...	...	...	...	1929	186	750 (I)	SR
Sloyne ...	...	...	...	...	1928	300	900 (I)	SR
Wallasey	...	...	...	...	1954	200	950 (I)	SR
Waterloo	...	...	...	...	1954	200	950 (I)	SR

BRITANNIA STEAM TOWING CO. LTD.

Clyneforth	...	...	...	...	1943	262	1,000 (I)	SR
Graigforth	...	...	...	...	1923	229	800 (I)	SR

ALEXANDRA TOWING CO. LTD.

FUNNEL and HOUSEFLAG: *See General Note at the beginning of this section.*

Cambrian	...	...	...	...	1960	163	890 (B)	M
Gower ...	...	...	...	...	1961	152	960 (B)	M
Talbot ...	...	...	...	...	1961	153	960 (B)	M

Also tugs at Southampton and Liverpool.

M.T. Gower. Alexandra Towing Co.
[*Fotoship*

S.T. Craigforth. Britannia Steam Towing Co.
[*Fotoship*

M.T. Newport. British Transport Docks. [*Fotoship*

THE ADMIRALTY

FUNNEL: *See General Note at the beginning of this section.*

Ocean Tug:								
Warden ...	...	...	...	...	1945	1,136	3,020	M(2)
Harbour Tug:								
Empire Netta ...	...	...	...	1946	295	800	SR

MILFORD HAVEN

THE MILFORD DOCKS CO.

FUNNEL: *Black with white band.*
HOUSEFLAG:

St. Govans	...	...	...	...	1901	60	350 (I)	SR

Also the smaller tugs **James Ward** and **Sidney Herbert**.

OVERSEAS TOWAGE & SALVAGE CO. LTD.

MILFORD HAVEN TUG SERVICES, LTD.

FUNNEL: *Yellow with black top and blue diamond bearing white letters "O T S"*
HOUSEFLAG: *Yellow with blue diamond bearing white letters " O T S".*

Britonia ...	...	...	...	...	1963	600	2,000 (I)	M
Marinia ...	...	...	...	...	1955	392	962 (B)	M
Sheilia ...	...	...	...	...	1940	52	450 (I)	M

R. & J. H. REA, LTD.

FUNNEL and HOUSEFLAG: *See General Note at the beginning of this section.*

Anglegarth*	...	...	...	...	1960	306	1,300 (B)	M
Dalegarth*	...	...	...	...	1960	306	1,300 (B)	M
Ramsgarth*	...	...	...	...	1964	306	1,300 (B)	M
Rathgarth*	...	...	...	...	1965	306	1,300 (B)	M
Reagarth*	...	...	...	...	1964	306	1,300 (B)	M
Stackgarth*	...	...	...	...	1959	306	1,300 (B)	M
Thorngarth*	...	...	...	...	1959	306	1,300 (B)	M

Also tug fleets at Southampton, Avonmouth, Cardiff and Barry.

* Kort Nozzle.

M.T. Warden. The Admiralty.
[*A. Duncan*

M.T. Britonia. Overseas Towage & Salvage Co.
[*John G. Callis*

S.T. North End. Alexandra Towing Co.
[*J. Clarkson*

4. Mersey & Manchester

R. ABEL & SONS, LTD.

FUNNEL: *Black with blue band bordered by two yellow bands.*
HOUSEFLAG:

Richard Abel	...	...	...	...	1944	54	220 (I)	SR

ALEXANDRA TOWING CO. LTD.

FUNNEL and HOUSEFLAG: *See General Note at the beginning of this section.*

Alexandra	...	...	...	...	1963	161	940 (B)	M
Alfred	...	...	...	...	1937	215	1,000 (I)	SR
Brocklebank	...	...	...	...	1965	142	1,200 (B)	M
Canning	...	...	...	...	1954	200	950 (I)	SR
Crosby	...	...	...	...	1937	215	1,000 (I)	SR
Egerton	...	...	...	...	1965	142	1,200 (B)	M
Formby	...	...	...	...	1951	237	1,200 (I)	SR
Herculaneum	...	...	...	...	1962	161	940 (B)	M
Hornby	...	...	...	...	1936	201	1,000 (I)	SR
Langton	...	...	...	...	1964	172	1,200 (B)	M
North Beach	...	...	...	...	1956	220	1,000 (I)	SR
North Buoy	...	...	...	...	1959	219	1,000 (I)	SR
North End	...	...	...	...	1957	215	1,000 (I)	SR
North Light	...	...	...	...	1956	206	1,000 (I)	SR
North Quay	...	...	...	...	1956	219	1,000 (I)	SR
North Rock	...	...	...	...	1956	206	1,000 (I)	SR
North Wall	...	...	...	...	1959	219	1,000 (I)	SR
Wapping	...	...	...	...	1936	201	1,000 (I)	SR

Also tug fleets at Southampton, Swansea and Port Talbot.

JOHNSTON WARREN LINES, LTD.

FUNNEL: *Dark red with black top, band and base.*
HOUSEFLAG: *Blue swallowtail with red and black striped disc in centre and white " F " in top of hoist.*

Foylemore	...	...	...	...	1958	208	1,270 (B)	M
Kilmore	...	...	...	...	1958	207	1,270 (B)	M
Rossmore	...	...	...	...	1958	206	1,270 (B)	M

J. H. LAMEY, LTD.

FUNNEL: *Red with black top and black " L " on broad white band.*
HOUSEFLAG: *White with deep red border and black " L " in centre.*

Anita Lamey	...	...	...	...	1920	172	1,000 (I)	SR
Edith Lamey	...	...	...	...	1942	147	400 (I)	SR
J. H. Lamey	...	...	...	...	1963	200	—	M
James Lamey	...	...	...	...	1928	260	950 (I)	SR
John Lamey*	...	...	...	...	1927	185	—	M
William Lamey	...	...	...	...	1959	166	1,000 (B)	M

*Rebuilt in 1957.

LIVERPOOL GRAIN STORAGE & TRANSIT CO. LTD.

FUNNEL:

HOUSEFLAG:

Ceres	...	...	...	...	...	1961	43	—	M

LIVERPOOL LIGHTERAGE CO. LTD.

FUNNEL: *Black with blue band bordered by two narrow white bands.*

HOUSEFLAG:

Kerne	...	...	...	...	1913	63	400 (I)	SR
Langbourne	...	...	...	...	1913	63	—	SR

LIVERPOOL SCREW TOWING & LIGHTERAGE CO.

H. EDWARDS

FUNNEL: *Yellow with narrow black top.*

HOUSEFLAG: *White with blue cock device in centre.*

Black Cock	...	...	...	...	1939	168	1,000 (I)	SR
Grebe Cock	...	...	...	...	1935	169	1,000 (I)	SR
Holm Cock	...	...	...	...	1934	167	1,000 (I)	SR
Storm Cock	...	...	...	...	1936	169	1,000 (I)	SR
Thistle Cock	...	...	...	...	1929	169	1,000 (I)	SR

NORTH WEST TUGS LTD.

Fighting Cock	...	...	...	...	1953	218	1,250 (I)	SR
Flying Cock	...	...	...	...	1960	165	—	M
Game Cock V	...	...	...	...	1953	218	1,250 (I)	SR
Heath Cock	...	...	...	...	1958	193	1,088 (B)	M
Peacock	...	...	...	...	1960	165	—	M
Weather Cock	...	...	...	...	1960	165	—	M
West Cock	...	...	...	...	1958	193	1,088 (B)	M

MANCHESTER SHIP CANAL CO.

FUNNEL: *Black with two closely spaced white bands.*

HOUSEFLAG: *Blue, white, blue, white, blue horizontal stripes (the centre blue stripe narrower than the others) with the blue letters "M S" and "C C" on the white.*

Daniel Adamson *	...	...	...	1903	175	583 (I)	SR(2)
M.S.C. Archer	...	...	...	1938	144	750 (I)	SR
M.S.C. Arrow †	...	...	...	1938	162	800 (B)	M
M.S.C. Badger	...	...	...	1939	144	750 (I)	SR

M.T. Rossmore. Johnstone Warren Lines. [*J. Clarkson*

S.T. James Lamey. J. H. Lamey Ltd. [*A. P. Oakden*

S.T. Langbourne. Liverpool Lighterage Co. [*J. Clarkson*

M.S.C. Bison ...	...	...	...	1939	144	750 (I)	SR
M.S.C. Firefly ...	...	...	...	1935	176	728 (I)	SR
M.S.C. Mallard	...	...	...	1939	131	770 (B)	M(2)
M.S.C. Merlin ...	...	...	...	1940	131	770 (B)	M(2)
M.S.C. Neptune	...	...	...	1941	131	770 (B)	M(2)
M.S.C. Nymph	...	...	...	1942	131	770 (B)	M(2)
M.S.C. Onset ...	...	...	...	1948	154	1,200 (B)	M(2)
M.S.C. Onward	...	...	...	1948	154	1,200 (B)	M(2)
M.S.C. Panther	...	...	...	1950	154	1,200 (B)	M(2)
M.S.C. Puma ...	...	...	...	1950	154	1,200 (B)	M(2)
M.S.C. Quarry	...	...	...	1951	154	1,200 (B)	M(2)
M.S.C. Quest ...	...	...	...	1952	154	1,200 (B)	M(2)
M.S.C. Ranger ...	...	...	...	1952	154	1,200 (B)	M(2)
M.S.C. Rover ...	...	...	...	1953	154	1,200 (B)	M(2)
M.S.C. Sabre ...	...	...	...	1956	147	1,290 (B)	M(2)
M.S.C. Sceptre	...	...	...	1956	147	1,290 (B)	M(2)
M.S.C. Scimitar	...	...	...	1956	147	1,290 (B)	M(2)
M.S.C. Sovereign	...	...	...	1957	147	1,290 (B)	M(2)
M.S.C. Talisman	...	...	...	1961	124	1,210 (B)	M(2)
M.S.C. Tarn ...	...	...	...	1962	124	1,210 (B)	M(2)
M.S.C. Undine	...	...	...	Building	—	—	—
Stanlow	...	...	...	1924	100	480 (I)	SR

Dredging Tugs: **M.S.C. Dainty, M.S.C. Daring, M.S.C. Daphne, M.S.C. Dawn, M.S.C. Deborah, M.S.C. Diana, M.S.C. Dido, M.S.C. Dolphin** and **M.S.C. Bennett.**

Bridgewater Department Tugs: **Appleton, Baddeley, M.S.C. Bantam I,** and **M.S.C Bantam II.**

*Tender.   †Rebuilt 1963.

REA LTD., and REA TOWING CO. LTD.

FUNNEL: *Red with black top separated by a narrow white band and with a white " R " in a white-bordered black diamond.*

HOUSEFLAG: *Red swallowtail with diamond device as on funnel.*

Applegarth	...	...	...	...	1951	231	1,120 (I)	SR
Aysgarth	...	...	...	...	1950	231	1,120 (I)	SR
Bangarth	...	...	...	...	1951	231	1,120 (I)	SR
Beechgarth	...	...	...	...	1964	200	1,350 (B)	M
Cedargarth	...	...	...	...	1961	230	1,350 (B)	M
Grassgarth	...	...	...	...	1953	231	1,120 (I)	SR
Hazelgarth	...	...	...	...	1959	230	1,680 (B)	M
Maplegarth	...	...	...	...	1961	230	1,350 (B)	M
Rosegarth	...	...	...	...	1954	231	1,120 (I)	SR
Throstlegarth ...	...	...	...	1954	231	1,120 (I)	SR
Willowgarth	...	...	...	...	1959	230	1,680 (B)	M

WESTMINSTER DREDGING CO. LTD..

FUNNEL: *Black with houseflag.*

HOUSEFLAG: *Divided diagonally from top of hoist, yellow over blue.*

WD Duck	...	...	...	...	1944	54	220 (I)	SR
WD Teal*	...	...	...	...	1943	54	—	M

Also the smaller tugs **WD Chick, WD Drake, WD Scoter** and **WD Snip.**

*Re-engined.

5. North West Coast

PORT OF PRESTON AUTHORITY

FUNNEL: *Black with shield of Preston coat-of-arms (light blue and white.)*
HOUSEFLAG: *Blue with coat of arms in centre.*

Charles Hearn	...	...	...	1959	139	740 (B)	M(2)
Frank Jamieson	...	...	...	1956	146	720 (B)	M(2)
Hewitt ...	...	...	...	1951	140	800 (B)	M(2)
John Herbert ...	...	...	...	1955	146	720 (B)	M(2)

FLEETWOOD

BRITISH TRANSPORT DOCKS

FUNNEL and HOUSEFLAG: *See General Note at the beginning of this section.*

Clevelys ...	...	...	...	...	1929	110	400 (I)	SR(2)
Landy II ...	...	...	...	...	1949	66	204 (I)	M(2)

HEYSHAM

JAMES FISHER & SONS LTD.

FUNNEL: *Yellow with black top and black " F " on broad white band.*
HOUSEFLAG: *White field with red border and large blue " F ".*

Fishershill	...	...	...	...	1946	292	850 (I)	SR
Fisherstown	...	...	...	...	1944	232	850 (I)	SR

Operators of Coastal Cargo Ships.

BARROW

BRITISH TRANSPORT DOCKS

FUNNEL and HOUSEFLAG: *See General Note at the beginning of this section.*

Rampside	...	...	...	...	1941	260	900 (I)	SR
Roa	...	...	...	...	...	1944	232	900 (I)	SR

WORKINGTON

THE WORKINGTON HARBOUR & DOCK CO. LTD.

FUNNEL: *Black with white band.*
HOUSEFLAG: *None.*

Solway ...	...	...	...	...	1943	232	900 (I)	SR

6. Clyde and West Coast of Scotland

IRVINE

IRVINE HARBOUR COMPANY

FUNNEL: *Maroon with black top.*

HOUSEFLAG:

Garnock*	...	...	...	...	1956	78	360 (B)	M

*Kort Nozzle.

ARDROSSAN

ARDROSSAN HARBOUR COMPANY

FUNNEL: *Black with houseflag on broad white band.*

HOUSEFLAG:

Seaway	...	...	...	...	1942	260	1,000 (I)	SR

CLYDE (GOUROCK, GREENOCK, GLASGOW AND DUMBARTON)

THE ADMIRALTY

FUNNEL: *See General Note at the beginning of this section.*

Harbour Tug:

Empire Ace	...	...	...	...	1942	275	850	SR

CLYDE SHIPPING CO. LTD.

FUNNEL: *Black*

HOUSEFLAG: *Blue pennant bearing white lighthouse device and white letters "C S C".*

(The hulls are distinguished by a broad ochre band with dummy black ports painted thereon)

Flying Demon	...	...	...	...	1964	120	—	M
Flying Dipper	...	...	...	...	1958	274	1,100 (B)	M
Flying Dolphin		...	...	...	1959	113	—	M
Flying Drake	...	...	...	...	1957	176	1,310 (B)	M
Flying Duck	...	...	...	...	1956	200	1,075 (B)	M
Flying Foam	...	...	...	...	1962	150	—	M
Flying Merlin	...	...	...	...	1951	261	1,150 (B)	SR
Flying Mist	...	...	...	...	1962	190	—	M
Flying Spray	...	...	...	...	1962	150	—	M
Flying Witch	...	...	...	...	1960	115	—	M
Flying Wizard	...	...	...	...	1960	115	—	M

S.T. Applegarth.
Rea Towing Co.
[*J. Clarkson*

M.T. Charles Hearn.
Port of Preston.
[*J. Clarkson*

S.T. Flying Spitfire.
Clyde Shipping Co.
[*John G. Callis*

STEEL & BENNIE LTD.

FUNNEL: *Black with broad white band.*

HOUSEFLAG: *Blue, white, blue horizontal stripes, with black " S & B " on white.*

Brigadier	...	...	...	...	1961	200	1,326 (I)	M
Campaigner	...	...	...	...	1957	248	1,384 (I)	M
Chieftain*	...	...	...	...	1930	223	858 (I)	M
Cruiser†	...	...	...	...	1953	304	1,750 (I)	M
Strongbow	...	...	...	...	1960	230	1,326 (I)	M
Thunderer	...	...	...	...	1958	208	1,040 (I)	M
Vanguard	...	...	...	...	1964	225	1,326 (I)	M
Warrior††	...	...	...	...	1935	259	1,211 (I)	M
Wrestler	...	...	...	...	1957	248	1,384 (I)	M

*Rebuilt 1957   †Rebuilt 1963   ††Rebuilt 1958

7. East Coast of Scotland

FORT AUGUSTUS
BRITISH WATERWAYS

FUNNEL: *Grey with black top.*

HOUSEFLAG: *Light blue with British Waterways device in yellow.*

Scott II	...	...	...	...	...	1931	59	36	SR

ABERDEEN
ABERDEEN HARBOUR BOARD

FUNNEL: *Black with letters "A.H.B." on broad yellow band between two narrow red bands.*

HOUSEFLAG: *None.*

Sea Griffon	...	...	...	...	1961	100	—	M
Sea Trojan	...	...	...	...	1961	105	—	M

DUNDEE
DUNDEE HARBOUR TRUST

FUNNEL: *Yellow with narrow black top.*

HOUSEFLAG: *Blue with armorial bearing in full colour superimposed on white St. Andrew's cross.*

Castlecraig	...	...	...	...	1951	139	660 (B)	M
Harecraig II	...	...	...	...	1951	261	1,180 (I)	SR

THE ADMIRALTY

FUNNEL: *See General Note at the beginning of this section.*

Harbour Tugs:								
Barbara ...	...	...	...	...	1963	38	400	M
Corgi ...	...	...	...	...	1964	152	1,320	M(2)
Empire Demon		...	...	...	1943	260	1,000	SR
Griper ...	...	...	...	...	1958	473	1,600	ME(PW)
Handmaid	...	...	...	...	1940	234	800	SR
Impetus ...	...	...	...	...	1940	234	800	SR
T.I.D. 164	...	...	...	...	1943	55	220	SR
T.I.D. 165	...	...	...	...	1943	55	220	SR

GRANGEMOUTH & FORTH TOWING CO. LTD.

FUNNEL: *Yellow with black top.*

HOUSEFLAG:

Dalgrain	...	...	...	...	1963	140	—	M
Dundas ...	...	...	...	...	1941	150	1,000	SR
Kerse ...	...	...	...	...	1923	214	800 (I)	SR
Roker ...	...	...	...	...	1904	119	380 (I)	SR(PW)
Zetland ...	...	...	...	...	1961	85	—	M

Roker is normally stationed at Methil.

LEITH DOCK COMMISSIONERS

FUNNEL: *Black.*

HOUSEFLAG: *Seal of the Port of Leith in full colour superimposed on a white St. Andrew's Cross on blue field.*

Craigleith*	...	...	...	...	1958	185	818 (B)	M
Martello*	...	...	...	...	1958	68	440 (B)	M
Mickry ...	...	...	...	...	1920	172	750 (I)	SR
Oxcar ...	...	...	...	...	1919	252	750 (I)	SR

*Kort Nozzle.

8. North East Coast

BLYTH HARBOUR COMMISSIONERS

FUNNEL: *Cream with black top.*

HOUSEFLAG: *Blue with words " Blyth Harbour Commission " in white.*

Chipchase*	...	...	...	...	1953	106	400 (I)	SR(2)
Cresswell	...	...	...	...	1960	374	—	M

*Tender.

BLYTH TUG CO. LTD.

FUNNEL: *Yellow with blue Maltese Cross.*

HOUSEFLAG:

Hillsider	...	...	...	...	1924	177	800 (I)	SR
Homer ...	...	...	...	...	1915	157	550 (I)	SR
Francis Batey	...	...	...	...	1914	151	750 (I)	SR

TYNE TUGS LTD.

FUNNEL: *Red with black top.*

HOUSEFLAG: *None.*

Tyne Tugs Ltd. is the operating company of tugs owned by three separate concerns as set out below:

France Fenwick Tyne & Wear Co. Ltd.

Alnwick ...	...	...	...	...	1955	119	1,086 (B)	M
Ashbrooke	...	...	...	...	1955	119	1,086 (B)	M
Bamburgh	...	...	...	...	1956	119	1,086 (B)	M
Beamish	...	...	...	...	1944	242	1,000 (I)	SR
Cullercoats	...	...	...	...	1898	181	700 (I)	SR
George V*	...	...	...	...	1915	224	1,086 (B)	M
Hendon ...	...	...	...	...	1924	241	950 (I)	SR
Marsden	...	...	...	...	1956	119	1,086 (B)	M
Wearmouth	...	...	...	...	1927	182	900 (I)	SR

Lawson-Batey Tugs Ltd.:

Eastsider	...	...	...	...	1924	175	600 (I)	SR
Applesider	...	...	...	...	1962	175	—	M
Joffre ...	...	...	...	...	1916	260	1,140 (I)	SR
Quaysider	...	...	...	...	1955	157	1,200 (B)	M
Roughsider	...	...	...	...	1958	143	750 (B)	M
Southsider	...	...	...	...	1940	239	1,000 (I)	SR
Tynesider	...	...	...	...	1942	262	1,000 (I)	SR
Westsider	...	...	...	...	1963	175	—	M

Ridley Tugs Ltd.:

Impetus ...	...	...	...	...	1954	141	750 (B)	M
Maximus	...	...	...	...	1956	141	750 (B)	M

*Rebuilt.

M.T. Warrior. Steel
& Bennie Ltd.
[*Steel & Bennie Ltd.*

S.T. Mickry. Leith
Dock Commis-
sioners.
[*D. R. Chesterton*

M.T. Bamburgh.
Tyne Tugs Ltd.
[*R. Sherlock*

FRANCE FENWICK TYNE & WEAR CO. LTD.

FUNNEL: *White with black top and a blue anchor on broad band of pale blue and white stripes.*

HOUSEFLAG:

Alnmouth	...	...	...	...	1962	170	—	M
Cleadon ...	...	...	...	...	1899	148	700 (I)	SR
Cornhill ...	...	...	...	...	1943	176	700 (B)	M
Dunelm ...	...	...	...	...	1964	150	—	M
Grangetown	...	...	...	...	1943	176	700 (B)	M
Prestwick	...	...	...	...	1955	119	1,086 (B)	M
Ryhope ...	...	...	...	...	1943	176	700 (B)	M

Also owners of tugs operating in the fleet of Tyne Tugs Ltd. at Newcastle.

RIVER WEAR COMMISSIONERS

FUNNEL: *Yellow with black top and black sextant.*

HOUSEFLAG: *None.*

Biddick ...	...	...	...	...	1944	54	220 (I)	SR
Pallion ...	...	...	...	...	1944	54	222 (I)	SR

SEAHAM HARBOUR

SEAHAM HARBOUR DOCK CO. LTD.

FUNNEL: *Black with broad red band.*

HOUSEFLAG: *None.*

Conservator	...	...	...	...	1925	96	387 (I)	SR
Eppleton Hall	...	...	...	...	1914	166	600 (I)	SR(PW)
Reliant ...	...	...	...	...	1907	156	—	SR(PW)

BRITISH TRANSPORT DOCKS

FUNNEL and HOUSEFLAG: *See General Note at beginning of this section.*

Hart	...	...	...	...	1958	145	1,200 (B)	M(2)
Seaton	...	...	...	...	1958	145	1,200 (B)	(2)
Stranton	...	...	...	...	1958	145	1,200 (B)	M(2)

TEES

TEES CONSERVANCY COMMISSION

FUNNEL: *Yellow with black top.*

HOUSEFLAG: *White with blue cross broken at centre by blue ring containing lettering " Tees Conservancy Commission" and surrounding armorial ship device.*

C. J. Archer	...	...	...	...	1913	64	160 (I)	SR
Francis Samuelson	...	...	...	1924	140	400 (I)	SR
Joanetta	...	...	...	...	1911	49	106 (I)	SR
John H. Amos	...	...	...	1931	202	500 (I)	SR(PW)
Lackenby	...	...	...	...	1946	54	220 (I)	SR
Wilton	...	...	...	...	1955	208	—	M

TEES TOWING CO. LTD.

WM. CROSSTHWAITE & SON

(Cross Line Tugs)

FUNNEL: *Red with black top and two widely spaced white bands.*

HOUSEFLAG:

Banbury Cross*	...	...	...	1958	106	750 (B)	M
Caedmon Cross	...	...	...	1953	132	882 (I)	M
Danby Cross	...	...	...	...	1961	120	—	M
Erimus Cross	...	...	...	...	1960	192	1,200 (B)	M
Fiery Cross†	...	...	...	...	1957	192	1,100 (B)	M
Golden Cross	...	...	...	...	1955	132	882 (I)	M
Hutton Cross*	...	...	...	1958	105	750 (B)	M
Ingleby Cross	...	...	...	...	1955	132	882 (I)	M
Marton Cross	...	...	...	...	1963	150	—	M

*Voith-Schneider Propellers.   †Kort Nozzle.

9. Humber & East Coast

BRITISH TRANSPORT DOCKS

FUNNEL and HOUSEFLAG: *See General Note at the beginning of this section.*

Foremost 87	...	...	...	...	1935	163	500 (I)	SR
Jones	...	...	...	...	1934	126	410 (I)	SR
Wyke	...	...	...	...	1956	62	480 (B)	M

JOHN DEHEER LTD.

FUNNEL: *Red with black top and black star.*

HOUSEFLAG:

Ian	...	...	...	...	1907	67	—	SR

Also the smaller tugs **Fairy** and **Rover**.

ELLERMAN'S WILSON LINE LTD.

FUNNEL: *Red with Black top.*

HOUSEFLAG: *White swallowtail pennant with red ball, flown with blue Ellerman pennant.*

(*These vessels have green hulls*)

Forto	...	...	...	...	1939	180	106 (I)	SR
Presto	...	...	...	...	1943	276	1,000 (I)	SR

PETER FOSTER & CO. LTD.

FUNNEL: *Black with broad silver band.*

HOUSEFLAG:

Larkspur	...	...	...	...	1919	135	465 (I)	SR
Overgarth	...	...	...	...	1907	97	320 (I)	SR

THE HULL STEAM TRAWLERS MUTUAL INSURANCE & PROTECTING CO. LTD.

FUNNEL: *Yellow with Black top.*

HOUSEFLAG: *None.*

Bernie ...	...	...	...	...	1944	54	220 (I)	SR
Aurora*	...	...	...	...	1963	50	385 (B)	M
Triton* ...	...	...	...	...	1964	50	385 (B)	M
Zephyr*	...	...	...	...	1964	50	385 (B)	M

*Voith-Schneider Tractor.

JOHN H. WHITAKER (HOLDINGS) LTD.

FUNNEL: *Black with separate red over green bands.*

HOUSEFLAG: *Pennant divided vertically red and green, with a white " W " on a white-bordered black disc on the red.*

Wilberforce	...	...	...	...	1920	45	—	SR

Also the smaller tug **Cawood**.

UNITED TOWING CO. LTD.

FUNNEL: *White with black top.*

HOUSEFLAG: *Blue pennant with blue " U " on five-pointed white star.*

Airman ...	...	...	...	...	1945	333	750 (I)	SR
Autocrat	...	...	...	...	1915	128	500 (I)	SR
Bargeman	...	...	...	...	1955	37	400 (I)	M
Bureaucrat	...	...	...	...	1916	137	550 (I)	SR

M.T. Lingo. Union
Lighterage Co.
[*W. Kitchenham*

M.T. Kingston Buci.
Shoreham Harbour
Trustees.
[*John G. Callis*

M.T. Adrianus
Letzer. Remorquage
Letzer S.A.
[*R. Sherlock*

UNITED TOWING CO. LTD. (*continued*)

Dockman	...	...	...	...	1949	68	650 (I)	M
Englishman	...	...	...	...	1965	500	4,110 (I)	M(2)
Foreman	...	...	...	...	1959	227	1,200 (I)	M
Guardsman	...	...	...	...	1946	329	750 (I)	SR
Handyman	...	...	...	...	1941	129	500 (I)	SR
Headman	...	...	...	...	1963	193	1,650 (I)	M(2)
Keelman	...	...	...	...	1958	37	400 (I)	M
Krooman*	...	...	...	...	1938	230	1,100 (I)	M
Lighterman	...	...	...	...	1954	37	450 (I)	M
Masterman	...	...	...	...	1964	229	1,650 (I)	M(2)
Merchantman	...	...	...	...	1964	230	1,500 (I)	M(2)
Motorman	...	...	...	...	1965	98	1,000 (I)	M(2)
Norman*	...	...	...	...	1929	222	1,100 (I)	M
Patrolman	...	...	...	...	1953	68	680 (I)	M
Pressman	...	...	...	...	1950	68	680 (I)	M
Prizeman*	...	...	...	...	1925	226	1,100 (I)	M
Rifleman	...	...	...	...	1945	333	750 (I)	SR
Riverman	...	...	...	...	1963	93	1,100 (I)	M
Scotsman†	...	...	...	...	1929	222	1,100 (I)	M
Serviceman††	...	...	...	...	1945	330	2,000 (I)	M
Tidesman	...	...	...	...	1963	98	1,000 (I)	M(2)
Tollman	...	...	...	...	1931	79	420 (I)	SR
Tradesman	...	...	...	...	1964	230	2,500 (I)	M(2)
Trawlerman	...	...	...	...	1963	98	1,000 (I)	M(2)
Tugman	...	...	...	...	1964	98	1,000 (I)	M(2)
Workman	...	...	...	...	1963	193	1,650 (I)	M(2)
Yorkshireman	...	...	...	...	1928	251	800 (I)	SR(2)

*Rebuilt 1965.   †Rebuilt 1964.   ††Rebuilt 1961.

GOOLE

BRITISH TRANSPORT DOCKS

FUNNEL and HOUSEFLAG: *See General Note at the beginning of this section.*

Alpha	...	...	...	...	...	1943	—	60 (B)	M

IMMINGHAM

Tugs owned by British Transport Docks (Hull), and by Messrs. J. H. Pigott & Son, Ltd., (Grimsby) operate at Immingham.

AIRE AND CALDER CANAL AND OTHER INLAND WATERWAYS

British Waterways operate small tugs on the Aire & Calder Canal from Goole, and with other operators from both Hull and Goole on the Rivers Humber, Ouse, Trent, etc.

GRIMSBY

BRITISH TRANSPORT DOCKS

Tugs based on Hull also operate on occasion at Grimsby.

GRIMSBY SALVAGE & TOWAGE CO. LTD.

FUNNEL: *White with black top and black letters " EX ".*

HOUSEFLAG:

Alfred Bannister	...	...	...	1964	40	—	M
Brenda Fisher ...	...	...	...	1955	52	360 (B)	M
William Grant	...	...	...	1963	52	—	M

J. H. PIGOTT & SON LTD.

FUNNEL: *Black with two silver bands.*

HOUSEFLAG:
(Black over grey hulls)

Lady Biddy	...	...	...	...	1930	109	600	SR
Lady Cecilia	...	...	...	...	1963	162	960 (B)	M
Lady Constance	...	...	...	1924	112	600	SR
Lady Elsie	...	...	...	...	1962	150	—	M
Lady Sarah	...	...	...	...	1909	197	750 (I)	SR
Lady Sybil	...	...	...	...	1964	130	—	M
Lady Thelma	...	...	...	...	1909	197	750 (I)	SR
Lady Theresa	...	...	...	1962	150	—	M
Lady Vera	...	...	...	...	1938	230	850 (I)	SR

BOSTON
PORT OF BOSTON AUTHORITY

FUNNEL: *White with black top.*

HOUSEFLAG: *None.*

Finlay	...	...	...	...	...	1914	73	250 (I)	SR

KINGS LYNN
KINGS LYNN CONSERVANCY BOARD

FUNNEL: *Yellow with black top.*

HOUSEFLAG: *Red cross on white field, with red letters " K L C B " in each quarter.*
(Grey hull with black bulwarks)

Conservator K. L.	...	...	...	1963	42	—	M

GREAT YARMOUTH
GREAT YARMOUTH PORT & HAVEN COMMISSIONERS

FUNNEL: *Yellow with black top.*

HOUSEFLAG:

Richard Lee Barber ...	...	...	1940	122	—	SR

GREAT YARMOUTH SHIPPING CO. LTD.

FUNNEL: *Yellow with black top.*

HOUSEFLAG: *Quartered diagonally, yellow over and under black, with letters " G Y S Co " in opposite colours in each quarter.*

The small steam tugs **Cypress** and **Gensteam**.

LOWESTOFT

BRITISH RAILWAYS

FUNNEL and HOUSEFLAG: *See General Note at the beginning of this section.*

Ness Point	...	...	...	...	1937	85	180 (I)	SR(2)

Also the smaller tug **Lound**.

IPSWICH

IPSWICH DOCK COMMISSION

FUNNEL: *Yellow with black top.*

HOUSEFLAG: *Blue with white letters " I D C ".*

River Orwell	...	...	...	...	1943	145	—	M

10. Northern Ireland and Eire

BELFAST

BELFAST HARBOUR COMMISSIONERS

FUNNEL: *Yellow with black top.*

HOUSEFLAG: *None.*

Sir Kenneth	...	...	...	...	1958	75	330 (B)	M(2)
Sir Milne	...	...	...	...	1945	54	220 (I)	SR
Somerton	...	...	...	...	1945	54	220 (I)	SR

JOHN COOPER (BELFAST) LTD.

FUNNEL: *Red with black top.*

HOUSEFLAG:

Audacious	...	...	...	...	1923	160	—	SR
Carrickfergus	...	...	...	...	1958	161	960 (B)	M
Cashel	...	...	...	...	1959	207	1,260 (B)	M
Clonmel	...	...	...	...	1959	207	1,260 (B)	M
Craigdarragh	...	...	...	...	Building	—	—	—
Cultra	...	...	...	...	1962	200	1,260 (B)	M
Meadow	...	...	...	...	1942	242	1,000 (I)	SR
Piper	...	...	...	...	1942	250	1,000 (I)	SR
Southampton	...	...	...	...	1910	227	—	SR

S.T. Gladstone.
Alexandra Towing
Co.   [*R. Sherlock*

M.T. Tradesman.
United Towing Co.
[*United Towing Co.*

M.T. Cultra. John
Cooper (Belfast)
Ltd.
     [*D. R. Chesterton*

JOHN KELLY, LTD.

FUNNEL: *Black with red over white over blue bands and black " K " on white.*

HOUSEFLAG: *Red swallowtail with blue border at top and bottom and large white " K " in centre.*

Lagan	...	...	...	...	...	—	50	—	SR

LONDONDERRY

THE ADMIRALTY

FUNNEL: *See General Note at the beginning of this section.*

Harbour Tugs:								
Empire Fred	...	...	...	...	1942	234	900	SR
Empire Rosa	...	...	...	...	1946	292	800	SR

DUBLIN

DUBLIN PORT & DOCKS BOARD

FUNNEL: *Yellow with black top*

HOUSEFLAG:

Anna Liffey	...	...	...	...	1917	217	800 (I)	SR
Ben Eader	...	...	...	...	1932	228	1000 (I)	SR
Cluain Tarbh	...	...	...	...	1963	286	—	M
Coliemore	...	...	...	...	1926	244	850 (I)	SR

CORK HARBOUR COMMISSIONERS

FUNNEL: *White with black top and base. The tenders carry a large plaque of the city arms on each side of the funnel.*

HOUSEFLAG: *Dark blue with City Arms surmounting white letters " C.H.C." in centre.*

Cill Airne (Killarney)*	...	...	1962	501	—	M(2)
Francis Hallinan	...	...	1944	296	—	SR
Richard Wallace	...	...	1944	54	220 (1)	SR

The first-named carries its name in Erse and English characters.

*Tender (non-towing).

JOHN COOPER (BELFAST) LTD.

Two tugs owned by this Company are normally stationed at Cork.

PORT & LINER SERVICES (IRELAND) LTD.

FUNNEL:

HOUSEFLAG:

Galway Bay*	...	...	...	1930	704	—	M

*Tender, 400 passengers.

11. Northern European Ports

(Only Ocean Tugs of the larger companies based
on ports from Cherbourg to Bremen are included)

CHERBOURG

SOC. CHERBOURGEOISE DE REMORQUAGE ET DE SAUVETAGE

FUNNEL: *Black with red band.*

HOUSEFLAG:

Cherbourgeoise No. 4	...	...	1930	296	—		SR(2)
Cherbourgeoise No. 5	...	...	1952	357	2,040 (B)		ME
Landemer	...	...	...	...	1903	546	850 (B)	SR

Also smaller harbour tugs and tenders.

LE HAVRE

SOC. DE REMORQUAGE ET DE SAUVETAGE "LES ABEILLES"

FUNNEL: *Black.*

HOUSEFLAG: *White with deep red border.*

Abeille No. 1	...	...	...	...	1959	101	650 (B)	M
Abeille No. 2	...	...	...	...	1960	106	650 (B)	M
Abeille No. 3	...	...	...	...	1956	102	650 (B)	M
Abeille No. 4	...	...	...	...	1939	326	1,300 (I)	SR
Abeille No. 5	...	...	...	...	1959	100	500 (B)	M
Abeille No. 6	...	...	...	...	—	—	500 (B)	M
Abeille No. 8	...	...	...	...	1946	252	850 (I)	SR
Abeille No. 9	...	...	...	...	1961	101	650 (B)	M
Abeille No. 11	...	...	...	...	1964	—	1,800 (B)	M
Abeille No. 12	...	...	...	...	1964	—	1,800 (B)	M
Abeille No. 13	...	...	...	...	1951	305	1,500 (B)	M
Abeille No. 15	...	...	...	...	1953	412	2,200 (I)	SR
Abeille No. 16	...	...	...	...	1958	126	650 (I)	M
Abeille No. 17	...	...	...	...	1961	152	1,000 (B)	M
Abeille No. 18	...	...	...	...	1961	151	1,000 (B)	M
Abeille No. 19	...	...	...	...	1961	152	1,000 (B)	M
Abeille No. 20	...	...	...	...	1957	351	1,800 (B)	M
Abeille No. 21	...	...	...	...	1961	101	500 (B)	M
Abeille No. 26	...	...	...	...	1960	323	1,800 (B)	M
Abeille No. 27	...	...	...	...	1956	235	—	M

Also two tenders and smaller harbour tugs. Some of the above work from Cherbourg.

SOC. DE REMORQUAGE L. THOMAS

FUNNEL:

HOUSEFLAG:

Capitaine Albert Ruault	...	...	1960	103	700 (B)	M
Capitaine Louis Thomas	...	...	1957	103	500 (B)	M

DUNKIRK (ALSO AT BOULOGNE AND CALAIS)

SOC. DE REMORQUAGE ET DE SAUVETAGE DU NORD

FUNNEL: *Red with black top and number of vessel in white figures.*

HOUSEFLAG: *White with red border and red " S R S N " in centre.*

Aventureux	...	...	...	...	1961	163	860 (B)	M
Brave	...	...	...	...	1953	240	1,850 (I)	SR
Complaisant	...	...	...	...	1953	239	1,850 (I)	SR
Farouche	...	...	...	...	1958	219	1,000 (B)	M
Gaillard	...	...	...	...	1943	191	600 (I)	SR
Glorieux	...	...	...	...	1955	101	650 (B)	M
Hardi	...	...	...	...	1959	359	2,100 (B)	M
Intrepide	...	...	...	...	1958	218	1,000 (B)	M
Jean-Bart	...	...	...	...	1956	716	3,000 (B)	M
Obstine	...	...	...	...	1943	191	600 (I)	SR
Puissant	...	...	...	...	1963	295	—	M
Resolu	...	...	...	...	1943	222	790 (I)	SR
Superbe	...	...	...	...	1959	101	650 (B)	M
Trapu	...	...	...	...	1952	282	1,220 (I)	SR
Triomphant	...	...	...	...	1956	101	650 (B)	M
Vaillant	...	...	...	...	1961	162	1,000 (B)	M

Also smaller harbour tugs.

OSTEND

BELGIAN STATE MARINE

FUNNEL: *Yellow with black top.*

HOUSEFLAG:

Zeearend	...	...	...	...	1957	509	—	ME
Zeeleeuw	...	...	...	...	1932	163	—	M
Zeetijger	...	...	...	...	1956	275	—	ME

Also a salvage vessel. (Operator of the Dover-Ostend service)

UNION DE REMORQUAGE ET DE SAUVETAGE S.A., etc.

Operating a consortium of the company's own fleet together with those of the S.A. de Remorquage a Helice (2), and Remorquage Letzer (3).

FUNNEL: (1) *Black with broad blue band between two narrow yellow bands.*
(2) *Black.* (3) *Black with broad white band bearing black letters "A L".*

HOUSEFLAG:

Adrianus Letzer	...	...	...	1961	136	1,000 (B)	M
Annick Gerling	...	...	...	1961	136	1,000 (B)	M
Baron de Maere	...	...	...	1939	105	620 (B)	M
Bernard Gerling	...	...	...	—	136	1,000 (B)	M
Brigitte Gerling	...	...	...	1962	136	1,000 (B)	M
Burgemeester Vandamme	...	...	...	1960	142	1,320 (B)	M
Catherine Letzer	...	...	...	1962	130	1,000 (B)	M
Christophe Letzer	...	...	...	1961	136	1,000 (B)	M
Dir. Fred G. Gerling	...	...	...	1945	151	650 (B)	M
Dominique Gerling	...	...	...	1963	136	1,000 (B)	M
Elisabeth Letzer	...	...	...	—	136	1,000 (B)	M
Francoise Letzer	...	...	...	—	136	1,000 (B)	M
Genevieve Letzer	...	...	...	1963	136	1,000 (B)	M
Georges Letzer	...	...	...	1945	298	2,200 (B)	M
Graaf Visart	...	...	...	1940	137	1,000 (B)	M
Jean Cl. Gerling	...	...	...	—	136	1,000 (B)	M
Jean Marie Gerling	...	...	...	1960	161	1,250 (B)	M
Laurent Letzer	...	...	...	1964	141	1,000 (B)	M
Leie	...	...	...	1953	155	450 (I)	SR
Leon Letzer	...	...	...	1946	116	400 (I)	SR
Lucile Gerling	...	...	...	1961	136	1,000 (B)	M
Marg. Gerling	...	...	...	1960	136	1,000 (B)	M
Martine Letzer	...	...	...	1960	161	1,750 (B)	M
Michel Gerling	...	...	...	1960	152	650 (B)	M
Olivier Gerling	...	...	...	1964	141	1,000 (B)	M
Philippe Gerling	...	...	...	—	136	1,000 (B)	M
Pierre V. Letzer	...	...	...	1961	110	750 (B)	M
Pipsy Letzer	...	...	...	1964	136	1,000 (B)	M
President Gerling	...	...	...	1927	156	600 (I)	SR
Raymond Letzer	...	...	...	1946	116	400 (I)	SR
Rolf Gerling	...	...	...	1943	122	1,000 (B)	M
Sabine Letzer	...	...	...	1963	136	1,000 (B)	M
Scaldis	...	...	...	1954	401	2,400 (B)	M
Yves Gerling	...	...	...	1964	136	1,000 (B)	M

Also smaller harbour and dock tugs and salvage craft.

ROTTERDAM

L. SMIT & CO's INTERNATIONALE SLEEPDIENST

FUNNEL: *Black with broad blue band. (Harbour tugs have broad red band.)*

HOUSEFLAG: *Divided vertically white and blue with a red diamond superimposed on centre.*

Barentsz-Zee	...	...	...	...	1957	526	1,650 (B)	M
Clyde	...	...	...	...	1957	820	4,500 (B)	M
Elbe	...	...	...	...	1959	820	4,500 (B)	M
Hudson	...	...	...	...	1964	663	4,000 (B)	M
Humber	...	...	...	...	1948	387	1,350 (B)	M
Ierse Zee	...	...	...	...	1933	836	4,500 (B)	M

M.T. Abeille No. 15. Soc. de Rem "Les Abeilles".
[*R. Sherlock*

M.T. Scaldis. Union de Remorquage S.A.
[*A. Duncan*

M.T. Jacob van Heemskerck. Bureau Wijsmuller.
[*A. Duncan*

Loire	...	...	...	...	...	1952	382	1,650 (B)	M
Maas	...	...	...	...	...	1954	253	1,350 (B)	M
Mississippi	...	...	...	...	1960	674	4,000 (B)	M
Noordzee	...	...	...	...	1949	335	1,000 (B)	M
Oceaan ...	...	...	...	...	1949	497	2,000 (B)	M
Oostzee	...	...	...	...	1952	497	2,000 (B)	M
Orinoco	...	...	...	...	1964	—	4,000 (B)	M
Poolzee	...	...	...	...	1946	328	1,000 (B)	M
Rode Zee	...	...	...	...	1949	500	2,000 (B)	M
Schelde ...	...	...	...	...	1958	423	2,500 (B)	M
Tasman Zee	...	...	...	...	1958	526	1,650 (B)	M
Thames ...	...	...	...	...	1961	624	4,000 (B)	M
Tyne	...	...	...	...	...	1944	386	1,350 (B)	M
Witte Zee	...	...	...	...	Building	—	—	—
Zwarte Zee	...	...	...	...	1963	793	9,000 (B)	M

Also a large fleet of coastal and harbour tugs, and a further fleet of harbour tugs owned by the associated N.V. Nieuwe Rotterdamse Sleepdienst and working in Rotterdam Europoort.

YMUIDEN AND AMSTERDAM

BUREAU WIJSMULLER, N.V.

FUNNEL: *Blue with black top separated by broad white band.*

HOUSEFLAG: *Red over white over blue stripes, the white broadened at the centre to contain the black letters " B W ".*

Cycloop ...	...	...	...	...	1957	244	1,200 (B)	M
Gelderland	...	...	...	...	1963	598	2,950 (B)	M
Groningen	...	...	...	...	1963	598	2,920 (B)	M
Hector ...	...	...	...	...	1958	206	1,200 (B)	M
Jacob van Heemskerck	...	...	...	1964	659	5,375 (B)	M
Nestor ...	...	...	...	...	1958	206	1,200 (B)	M
Simson ...	...	...	...	...	1958	206	1,200 (B)	M
Stentor ...	...	...	...	...	1958	206	1,200 (B)	M
Titan ...	...	...	...	...	1955	244	1,200 (B)	M
Willem Barendsz	...	...	...	1963	659	5,375 (B)	M

Also smaller harbour tugs and salvage craft.

HAMBURG

BUGSIER REEDEREI– UND BERGUNGS– A.G.

FUNNEL: *Black with broad white band.*

HOUSEFLAG: *Quartered diagonally red over white over blue, and with letters " B R B A " in each quarter. (White letters on red and blue, blue letters on white).*

Alk	...	...	...	...	...	1943	138	—	M
Atlantic ...	...	...	...	...	1959	773	5,000 (I)	M(2)
Atlas	...	...	...	...	...	1960	250	2,500 (I)	M
Danzig	...	...	...	...	...	1938	244	2,200 (I)	M
Hermes ...	...	...	...	...	1956	293	1,900 (I)	M(2)
Pacific	...	...	...	...	...	1962	1,093	8,500 (I)	M
Seefalke ...	...	...	...	...	1924	619	3,000 (I)	M(2)
Thor	...	...	...	...	...	1942	208	—	SR
Wotan	...	...	...	...	...	1940	729	2,600 (I)	M(2)

Also many smaller harbour tugs and salvage vessels. Operators also of Ocean Freighters.

FAIRPLAY SCHLEPPDAMPF. REEDEREI G.m.b.H.

FUNNEL: *Black with broad white band bearing red four-pointed star super-imposed by a similar blue star.*

HOUSEFLAG: *White with star device as on funnel.*

Fairplay II	...	...	...	...	1959	136	1,000 (B)	M
Fairplay IV	...	...	...	...	1954	127	950 (1)	M
Fairplay VI	...	...	...	...	1957	136	1,000 (B)	M
Fairplay VII	...	...	...	...	1943	175	1,000 (1)	SR
Fairplay X*	...	...	...	...	Building	—	—	—
Fairplay XI	...	...	...	...	1963	173	1,750 (1)	M
Fairplay XIV	...	...	...	...	1955	136	1,000 (B)	M

Also smaller harbour tugs.   * Kort Nozzle

BREMEN

UNTERWESER REEDEREI

FUNNEL: *Black with houseflag on broad white band.*

HOUSEFLAG: *Divided diagonally red over and under blue, with white letters " U. R. A. G " in each quarter.*

Berne	...	...	...	...	1959	128	1,000 (B)	M
Blexen	...	...	...	...	1963	152	1,700 (B)	M
Blumenthal	...	...	...	...	1963	152	1,700 (B)	M
Brake	...	...	...	...	1954	114	1,320 (B)	M
Bremen	...	...	...	...	1952	133	1,600 (B)	M
Bremerhaven	...	...	...	...	1904	105	1,065 (B)	M
Elsfleth	...	...	...	...	1961	120	1,300 (B)	ME(2)
Farge	...	...	...	...	1954	114	1,320 (B)	M
Gropelingen	...	...	...	...	1959	105	750 (B)	M
Hemelingen	...	...	...	...	1959	105	750 (B)	M
Hoheweg	...	...	...	...	1960	290	3,200 (B)	M(2)
Robbenplate	...	...	...	...	1963	265	3,200 (B)	M
Rotesand	...	...	...	...	1961	292	3,200 (B)	M(2)
Stedingen	...	...	...	...	1962	149	1,000 (B)	M

Also many smaller harbour tugs.

M.T. Tyne. Internationale Sleepdienst. [*A. Duncan*

M.T. Pacific. Bugsier Reederei.
[*A. Duncan*

M.T. Hermes. Bugsier Reederei.
[*John G. Callis*